han **stop**
being broke

alastair
dorsett

what the
f*ck is
investing?

Disclaimer

The information contained in this book is not intended as, and shall not be understood or construed as, financial advice. I am not an attorney, accountant or financial advisor, nor am I holding myself out to be. The information presented in this book is not a substitute for financial advice from a professional who is aware of the facts and circumstances of your individual situation.

I have done my best to ensure that the information provided in this book is accurate and valuable. Regardless of anything to the contrary, nothing in this book should be understood as a recommendation that you should not consult a financial professional to address your particular circumstances. I expressly recommend you seek advice from a professional before making any investment decisions.

*What the f*ck is investing?*

Copyright © 2021 by Alastair Dorsett

Table of Contents

"**Someone** is sitting
in the shade today
because **someone**
planted a tree
a long time ago"

W a r r e n   B u f f e t

Introduction

What would you do if you were to win the lottery tomorrow?

Would you get up, get dressed and drive to work? Would you clock in and carry on working? Or would you call your boss and say you won't be in today... or ever again?

Who wouldn't want the option of giving up the rat race and doing something they really enjoy?

Unfortunately winning the lottery is almost impossible and so it probably isn't going to ever allow you to do that!

If you dream of quitting your job and doing something more fulfilling, you are not alone. We are taught that we should get an education, get a career and then work for forty years. We do this just to build enough of a pension to retire. You spend your best years working in a job you probably hate so you can quit it when you are too old to do anything else.

The problem with relying on a job to become financially independent is this; in your job you get paid based on how many hours you work. Your capacity to make money from your job is directly linked to the number of hours you can work. The number of hours you can work is fixed. You cannot create more time and so relying solely on your job limits your ability to make money.

Fortunately, there are things you can do now to achieve your own financial independence much earlier than you might expect.

All it takes is a change in your thinking. You need to remove that link in your brain between your time and your money.

The way to do this is through investing.

Your capacity to earn money from investing is unlimited. Most importantly, investing allows you to earn money passively without having to actively work for it. You really can earn money while you sleep!

Whilst it is easy to say "Just invest your money", you might not have disposable income to invest. Even if you do, you might not know how to invest it. The world of investing is geared against individual investors; it is made to look more complicated than it actually is.

In the following pages, you will learn everything you need to get started in the world of investing. You will find easy to implement tools and strategies that will help you manage your money better and improve your decision making. This will ultimately help you carve your path to financial independence.

The first step to financial independence is in your hands right now.

Think of it this way; what if you were allowed to make just ten investment decisions in your whole life?

You would more than likely become very wealthy.

Why?

Because you would read every single book and resource about investing that you could. Investing a couple of hours in a book would be absolutely insignificant in comparison to the money you can gain by being more informed, making better decisions and not losing money.

Chapter 1:
Get your house in order

Learning and implementing good financial habits in your life is the first thing you need to do if you want to reach your financial goals. There is little point in investing your money if you are paying interest on debts at the same time. Equally, you will never be able to invest money if you spend every penny you earn. Most people think they need to earn more money to become wealthy. Whilst that certainly helps, being more disciplined with the money you do earn can actually be just as powerful. It is one of the few things you can do that is in your direct control. You can't easily control whether you get a pay rise but you can certainly control what you do with the cash you already earn.

Small steps achieve big goals

When trying to achieve a goal that might look complicated or time consuming, a good strategy to employ is to simply take small, regular steps towards that goal. Trying to do too much at once can often lead to becoming frustrated or burned out. Nothing worth achieving happens quickly and gathering knowledge is no different. If you want to get in shape, going to the gym once for an hour will not get you there. Similarly if you want to be a successful investor, researching investments for one hour will not make you successful.

The best way to succeed in either goal is to make a habit of regularly working on the goal. If you want to get in shape, working out three or four times a week over months or years will move you towards that target. The more workouts you do over more time, the better shape you will be in. The same is true for your financial success. If you spend small amounts of time researching, learning and planning regularly, you are much more likely to find good opportunities and make good decisions.

The desire to get rich quick clouds judgement and this leads to making poor decisions and losing money. If the average investor put the same effort and thought into picking an investment as they did for a house or a car, the average investor would achieve much higher returns.

Another problem is that most people simply aren't taught how to manage their own money. It is something most

Steps to improving your finances

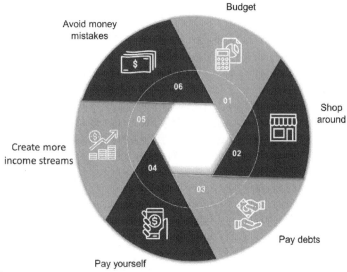

 What the **f*ck** is investing?

of us are not taught in school. Take the following steps to get yourself on stable financial ground before starting your investment journey.

Step 1: Budget

The first thing any of us should do to make the most of your income is to make a budget. Not having a budget is like trying to build a piece of IKEA furniture without the instructions; you might after a long struggle get something that resembles a piece of furniture. Sooner or later though, it's going to fall apart.

One of the goals of budgeting as you've probably guessed is to reduce your outgoings. The great thing about reducing your outgoings is that doing so is entirely within your control. Don't believe that your monthly outgoings are fixed, they are not. Energy bills are not fixed, insurance bills are not fixed and mortgages aren't even fixed. You will be surprised at just how much unnecessary spending you can cut out. What is also often overlooked is that reduced living costs also mean you need less money to be financially independent. With lower bills to pay, you need less income to pay them and therefore a smaller investment pot will be needed to create that income. You can reach that goal much faster if you stick to your budget. Think of your budget as the instructions on how to achieve your financial goals.

To make a budget, first you need to know where every penny goes every month. Luckily you don't actually have to manually trawl through your bank account statements each month, meticulously adding each transaction to an excel spreadsheet and categorising them. I said budgeting was easy and it is. There are countless clever mobile apps people have created that can do this for you without you having to lift a finger. A lot of these are free and some banks even have them built into their online banking app. Search for a budgeting app, find one you like and give it a try. I have listed my favourite budgeting apps on www.wtfinvesting. com/budgeting-apps. Any legitimate ones that you can link securely to your bank account are the best ones to try. They will recognise every outgoing and incoming transaction from your bank accounts each month and categorise them for you.

When you can see exactly where your money is going, you must prioritise your spending. Essential spending is used to sustain yourself and your family. Things like utilities, housing, food, transport, debt payments, child care and clothing are essential spending. Non-essential spending is anything that does not sustain yourself or your family. These are things like eating out, designer clothes, gambling or anything not covered under essential spending.

Step 2: Shop around

One of the easiest ways of really compressing your outgoings that surprisingly few people actually practise is shopping around for a better deal. You might shop around for some things, such as a car or a phone but you can also shop around for every single one of your outgoing bills. It is such a powerful thing to do and it actually takes so little effort once you know how.

I really saw the impact of not shopping around a few years ago when I looked over some bills for my mum. I was shocked when her house insurance renewal letter came in. The renewal quote was around £750. I didn't know whether this was good or not until I went online to check. I went onto a well-known price comparison website and copied in the same details that were on the renewal quote. The lowest price that came back for the exact same cover was around £75! That is ten times the

What the **f*ck** is investing?

difference! The same insurer even quoted a price that was around a fifth of their original renewal quote. The cost of not keeping on top of every bill can be substantial. If you simply pay the renewal quote every year when it comes in, you can be sure that you are getting a bad deal.

Taking your utility bills as another example, one of the big price comparison websites claims that people switching to one of their five cheapest tariffs saved an average of £375 per year! For car insurance the same website claims 50% of people could save up to £283 per year! You can easily shop around for telecoms, mortgages, credit cards and many different types of insurance and you absolutely should. If I offered you several hundred pounds to spend an hour entering a few details into a website, would you turn it down? Of course you wouldn't!

Another bonus of shopping around is that there are often extra incentives to shop around on top of cash savings. When I switch a service, I usually get a gift card or cashback on top of actually saving money. It took me over ten years to switch my bank account. I could never be bothered and didn't see any benefits to it. This year I finally switched and my new bank kindly gave me £275 cash for doing so! Why had I waited for so long? My new bank even provides a better service than my last one and it only took me about an hour in total to do. Banks often do these cash incentives for switching and you could easily make a couple of hundred pounds a year by switching regularly.

If you add up the cost of not shopping around for all these services every year, it is actually staggering. I challenge you to dedicate an hour this week to look into all these services you have. Get some quotes and just see how much money you are wasting. Note down how much you can save and also gain in cashback and gift cards. Go to www.wtfinvesting.

com/comparison-sites to find some of my favourite comparison sites. I can guarantee you will find money to be saved especially if you don't usually shop around.

Whilst you are looking at your outgoings, now is the perfect time to look at all those subscriptions you have coming from your accounts every month. Do you really need to have amazon prime, Netflix, Disney + as well as a full Sky TV package? If you counted the hours you spent on each, you would realise two things. First, you use one of these services much more than the others and second you only have some of these subscriptions because they seem too difficult to cancel! Cut these back to what you actually use. I found that I had all of these subscriptions and yet I only ever used one or two of them. It was an easy thing to cut out of the monthly outgoings.

Another type of subscription to watch out for is the free trial that you forgot to cancel. If you forgot to cancel it or didn't know how to cancel it, you don't need it. If you don't know how to cancel these services, simply search for their customer service email address online and email them asking them to cancel your account. They'll try to convince you to stay but just say no!

Step 3: Pay debt

With some discipline, you can cut your non-essential spending right back. As we have seen though, you can also cut your essential spending by reducing how much your debt costs. One way of doing this is by clearing your high interest short term debt. By short term debt, I don't mean your mortgage; I mean your credit cards, personal loans and anything else with a high interest rate. Now you might laugh and say that it's easy for me to say that but much harder to put into practise. All I can say is that

I know how hard getting out of debt can be but it can be done if you prioritise your spending correctly. You have to address it and tackle it head on.

Look at each debt you have and the interest rate on each and every type of debt. List each debt in order with the highest interest debt at the top. Ensure you make minimum payments on the other debts but focus as much money as you can on the highest interest debt first. When it's paid off, tackle the next highest then next and so on.

If you have debts, then non-essential spending should be cut right back to zero. You need to aggressively shop around to reduce the rest of your spending. If you have a credit card and a reasonable credit score, it might be possible for you to transfer your credit card balance to a lower or even zero interest card for a period of time. Make sure you check all the fees involved and ensure it's cheaper before you try it.

Debt is like fire and should be treated as such; if you are not very careful you could easily get burned. I used the balance technique myself before I started investing to clear my credit card debt without paying any interest. I stopped paying up to £50 per month in interest simply by transferring my balances to a zero interest card, allowing me to pay the balance much sooner.

Above all, remember the easiest way to get out of debt is not to have any in the first place. Debt is expensive and you should avoid it in the future.

Step 4: Pay yourself

Now that you know exactly where your money is going every month and you have reduced your outgoings as much as possible, you can look at what you can do with what's left. The first thing you should do with this spare money is to pay yourself. In other words, take a portion of this and either save it or invest it. Think of it as paying yourself at some point in the future.

As a rule of thumb, I normally have about six months' worth of living expenses saved as easily accessible cash in case an emergency reveals itself. Things like a car breakdown cost money and do happen. The last thing you want to have to do is to either sell an investment or take on debt to pay for an emergency. Six months' worth of living expenses will also give me protection in case I lost my income for example. I would have time to liquidate investments if necessary in order to sustain myself and my family until my income is restored again.

The 2020 pandemic is an example of how you should prepare for events that you just can't predict and that you and your family's financial security should be carefully considered. Once you have built up an appropriate savings cushion, you can then start putting this part of your budget towards investments.

After you have paid yourself you can set aside a budget for non-essential spending. I wouldn't stop going for the occasional meal out or treating the kids to a day out. All I would say though is that you create a budget for this type of spending and stick to it. Remember that the more money you spend on designer trainers, the less money you have working for you.

Step 5: Create more than one income stream

Once you have your finances in a good position, you can start devoting more energy to creating more streams of income. Most of us rely on our jobs for income. As we have seen with the 2020 pandemic and the countless job losses this has caused, it is apparent that you should not rely on one source of income to support yourself. The main subject of this book of course is investing; investing is just one way of creating more sources of income. Investing can bring in both dividend income, capital gains income and interest income. In the following chapter, I explain what the seven types of income are. Consider each type of income and start thinking of ways you can raise an income stream from each category. It doesn't matter how small the income stream is; if you can think of a way of bringing in extra income from a different category, you should try it. The more you do it, the better you will get at it. Chapter 2 will explain the seven types of income you can generate.

Step 6: Avoid these money mistakes

There are many small mistakes you can make with your money day to day that might seem insignificant individually but if you add them all up, they will cost you a lot in the long term. To be financially successful, often you have to keep your ego in check. How many mistakes in the list below have you made? How much have they cost you if you are completely honest with yourself? Simply being aware of the mistakes you have made is often enough to stop you from making them again. Be honest with yourself and recognise where you are holding yourself back.

Keeping up with the Joneses

One big mistake I've made myself but have also seen a lot of other people make is what is known as "Keeping up with the Joneses". This is when you see someone you know buying something new like a car or the latest phone and then feel the need to "keep up" by buying something similar yourself. It's something we've all done but it has the effect of making us spend money we don't need to and didn't plan to. When I see a brand new car straight out of the showroom, I try to think about the money lost when the car drives off the forecourt and not how nice the car is! Just remember to leave your ego behind and live within your means. Think of the opportunity cost of this kind of spending and this will help. Someday you might be driving that new car off the forecourt but not before you've met your goals and certainly not by using debt.

Making money decisions based on poor information or pressure

There are industries built upon encouraging us to part with our money. Making money decisions under pressure is never a good idea and that is exactly why some sales people use pressure to get you to part with your money. Taking out a financial product such as a loan or insurance without good information can result in getting a bad deal. You could end up paying high interest rates or buying insurance that doesn't meet your needs for example. If you don't feel comfortable with a financial decision because you feel under pressure or because you don't understand it; don't make the decision. Remove yourself from the situation and seek advice or guidance from someone who does understand it and that you can trust.

Prioritising the wrong debt

When you have debt, it is important to know what the cost of that debt is to you. You should prioritise paying off your highest interest debt first. This way you can minimise the total interest you pay and clear your debts quicker.

Missing payments

Lack of discipline when paying your debts can be extremely costly. Missing a single payment by a day can have high costs in terms of both fees and interest. Missing payments also has a negative impact on your credit report which in turn will make future debt more expensive or hard to get.

Not defining the difference between wanting and needing

You can make the mistake of overspending when you don't make the differences between your wants and needs clear. If you dropped your phone and cracked the screen for example, you might think "I've had this phone a few years; I need a new phone now anyway". In this case, you might end up going out and spending £1000 on buying a new phone. In reality, you just need to get the screen repaired which costs much less than £1000.

Depending on one income source

You can never predict the future and that is exactly why you need to have back up plans in case things happen that you didn't predict. The global pandemic in 2020 is a prime example. Hundreds of thousands of people lost their jobs as a result of the economic damage done during the pandemic. A majority of people rely on their jobs to support themselves and their families. This means a huge number of people will have been struggling to support themselves and their families because the source of income they relied on had gone. If you lost your job tomorrow, how long would it take before you couldn't pay your rent or your mortgage? How long could you stay afloat with no job? If you run the numbers, I'm sure you'll find them worrying unless you have another source of income.

You spend more than you make

This is the classic mistake we're all guilty of; we've spent more in a month than we've earned. Whilst this is completely fine every now and then, life events happen. You might even book a well-earned break or treat yourself every now and then. It only becomes a problem if you make a habit of it. If you consistently make a habit of overspending, you will never be able to build your investments. Even worse, do it for too long and you risk falling into debt.

You spend more when you earn more

When you get a promotion in your job, what's the first thing you think about? You think about what you could buy with that extra money. Over time, as your wages increase, your expenses increase too. It can even be so gradual that you hardly notice it. When your non-essential spending increases with your earnings like this, it's called life style creep or life style inflation. Whether it's a new car, new phone or an extra holiday, life style creep is something you should try to limit if you want to build your wealth. Someone earning $50,000 per year who invests $10,000 per year would quickly become wealthier than someone who earns $100,000 per year but invests nothing. Over a period of time, the person who earned $50,000 per year would be able to retire and the other person would have to keep working.

Not having emergency savings

If you invest a portion of your income every month but put nothing in your savings account, you could be making a costly mistake. What would happen if a large expense came up that you didn't foresee or plan for? You might have to liquidate some of your investments at short notice in order to pay this expense. This could cost you a lot

What the **f*ck** is investing?

of money. What if some of your shares had taken a dip recently and you have to realise that loss by selling to pay for this unforeseen expense? It is good practise to keep some money aside that you can access easily in case these things come up.

Not having a will

No one wants to think about their own death and this is why so few of us have wills. The consequences of this could be that your assets go to people you hadn't intended if you die. Your family members could end up breaking apart fighting over your estate. I've seen it happen first hand, things get messy when people die without a will. If you have assets you want to pass to your loved ones, put a bit of time aside and get a will sorted.

Using credit, not cash

How many times have you bought something you wanted with credit because you didn't have the cash available right then? How much more did that cost you than buying it in cash? You might say "Aha, but it was interest free credit!" Well I would say you that there is no such thing as interest free. Don't believe it for a second, you are paying for it somewhere. Either the product is overpriced to include the cost of the credit or they have sold you more than you had originally wanted. Either way, you've got a bad deal.

If you had taken the time to save the money in cash for that purchase, would you still honestly have made the purchase? You see numbers on a screen and it is easy to lose a sense of the actual cost. £50 a month over two years for the latest phone seems like a bargain but if you had £1200 cash in your hand instead, would you make that purchase as quick? Save up the cash to buy things instead of using credit, you might find when you have that cash in your hand that you'd rather keep the cash. Equally sometimes you might find that you still want or have to buy the product. In that case, go ahead; at least you haven't lost anything.

Chapter 2:
The **seven types** of income

You can put the seven types of income into two groups; active income and passive income. Active income is money that you get in exchange for doing something. Your job is an example of this. You do work or provide a service and get paid based on how many hours you spend doing it. Passive income however is not directly related to the amount of time you spend generating it. It still requires effort at the start to get the income stream going but once started; passive income will generate even when you're not working on it. Owning a stock is a good example of this. You invest your time researching the stock and then invest your money. The stock then pays you for owning it through either capital gains or dividends or both. You will find that nearly all wealthy people will have more than one income source and most will have both active and passive income sources. You should aim to replicate this and build income from as many of the following sources as you can.

Earned income

Earned income is something you will be familiar with. It is one of the income types we are taught about in school. Earned income is something you get from your job or careers. Your earned income is directly related to the number of hours you work. As such your ability to earn income in this way is physically limited. Time is the only resource you have that you cannot get more of. There are only ever going to be twenty-four hours in a day, you are never going to be able to make more hours.

You could work more hours every day but then of course other parts of your life will suffer. The highest paid jobs in the world will expect you to sacrifice much more of your life and that is one of the reasons they are highly paid.

Another thing to consider is that earned income is the most heavily taxed income in most countries. In the UK, the tax rate starts at 20% and rises with the income you earn. Clearly, it would be advantageous to reduce the tax you pay. Do this by earning money through income streams that are taxed less. Whilst most of us will have to rely on our earned income to support ourselves and our family initially, the goal is to build income from other sources to make our earned income less critical to supporting your live. When you achieve this, you can then pursue earned income sources you are passionate about or you could reduce the number of hours you spend earning income altogether.

Interest

Interest is also something you will be familiar with. Interest is income you can earn on money you put into a savings account. A bank will pay you interest to store your cash with them; they will then lend that money out to other people. These people will then pay the money back to the bank after a period of time as well as paying the bank interest. If you have ever seen the movie "It's a wonderful life", George explains this concept to his customers when they all come to his bank at once to withdraw their money after hearing rumours that the bank had no money. It led to the classic line "The bank doesn't have your money, it's in Bills house and Teds house". George was trying to explain the relationship between savers, borrowers and banks. A "run on the bank" as seen in the movie is a thing of the past now thanks to financial compensation schemes which promise to guarantee savings in some countries.

When looking into earning interest, you need to pay attention to the interest rate you will get. It is not a good idea to keep all your money in a savings account when interest rates are low. The S&P 500 has gained on average 9.2% a year since the year 1920. Why then would you put your money in a savings account that pays 0.25% interest? Obviously risk is one reason you might prefer savings instead but there are still low risk investments that can return much more than 0.25%.

So how are interest rates set? Central banks set interest rates for bank to bank lending and this has huge knock on impacts across our economy. Low interest rates are intended to lower the cost of borrowing for businesses and consumers. The thought behind this is that as a result, people will have more money which will encourage them to spend money and boost the economy. The downside of this is that the people relying on savings will get lower returns. There is also a risk that with more debt created during low interest times, the risk of defaults rises when interest rates go back up again.

Another part of the picture to consider here is inflation. Inflation is the reduction in the buying power of your money every year. It is why your grandparents always say that they could buy more for their money in their day. It is because they could. There are a few causes of inflation; it can be driven by both governments and consumers.

Higher demand for goods, services and homes as well as rising production costs causes prices to rise. Governments also influence inflation through their monetary policies; changes to tax rates and the supply of money both have big effects on inflation rates.

Inflation in the UK has averaged 2.51% a year since 1981. This means that your pound is worth 2.51% less each year. If you save your money in a savings account that earns 0.25% interest a year, it means that your money will have 2.26% less buying power each year. This might not sound like much but when you stretch that out over a long period of time; it means your money will half in value every thirty years. If you are planning on investing for your retirement, a savings account is clearly not going to get you there! Any interest you do earn is also taxable if it is over a certain limit unless your money is held in a tax efficient account. This makes the situation even worse! Easy access savings accounts are however a convenient way of storing limited funds for emergencies. As I've said previously, about 6 months' worth of expenses should be kept within reach in a savings account.

Dividend income

Dividend income is a passive income source where an investor is paid just for owning a stock. When a company makes a profit, they sometimes invest some of that profit back into their business in order to grow the business. Some businesses however will take some of that profit and give it back to their owners in the form of dividend payments. The person who holds shares will get paid a set amount per share that they own. This means that the more shares they own, the more money they will get paid. Dividend payments are often shown as a percentage of the share price. This is known as the dividend yield. A good dividend

What the **f*ck** is investing?

yield would be between 4% and 6% but they will usually vary with market conditions and interest rates. A dividend yield of 4% simply means that if you owned £100 worth of shares, you would get a return of £4 per year. If the dividend rate offered by a company is lower than interest rates, then there would be less incentive for investors to buy the shares. This is because investors could get better returns for less risk by using savings accounts. This type of income is taxable in most countries unless the shares the dividends are paid on are held within a tax efficient account. This is one of the reasons tax efficient accounts such as the UK Stocks and Shares ISA are powerful tools. I talk in more detail about building an investing strategy based on dividends later in chapter five and more about account types in chapter six.

Capital gains income

Capital gains income is generated when an asset is sold for a greater price than it was bought for. Capital gains income is usually a passive income source. Most of the time the owner of the asset does not need to do anything for the asset to rise in value. This is not true in all cases. Real estate for example, can go up in value if the owner puts work into improving it in some way. There are many ways of making capital gains income. Assets such as stocks, bonds, precious metals, real estate and even art are considered capital assets. When you buy shares and then sell them for a higher price than you bought them for, you will have made a capital gain. Much like the other types of income we have discussed, the tax man also wants a cut of your capital gains. Luckily just like some of the other income types, in most countries there is a tax free allowance for capital gains. It is also again possible to protect your stocks and shares from capital gains tax by holding them in your tax efficient account if you have one.

Profit

Profit income is what businesses make when they sell goods or services for a higher price than it cost to produce them. If a bakery sells a cake for £10 when it cost them £8 to make it, they have made £2 profit. Profit income as you can see is very much an active income source. You will have to do work in order to earn profit. The amount of work required however can vary. It is possible to make more money for the time you put into your business than from the time you put into your job. This is why moving from relying solely on earned income to profit income is what some people aspire to. If you are reading this, the chances are, you are one of those people. Starting your own business alongside your day job is a good way to start your journey to making profit income. The tax rules around businesses are a much more complex subject than for the other income sources. There are no tax free wrappers like there are for some other income sources. If you want to start a business, you need to make sure the tax man gets his cut.

Rental income

Rental income is made when you rent a property that you own to a tenant. Owning property can attract not only rental income but also capital gains income. The problem is that buying property takes a lot of capital. Even putting down a deposit and borrowing money to then buy property requires a large capital outlay, usually at least 25% of the value of the property. You will then have to pay interest on the loan you take out which will reduce the income you can make from the property.

Landlords also have the extra risks and headaches that come with tenants. Tenants could stop paying rent or they could damage the property. You would then have to

What the **f*ck** is investing?

go through lengthy and costly court proceedings to evict them. Buying property is not a passive income source; it will require work and further investment to keep the property running smoothly. Given the large capital outlay required just to start earning this type of income, it will be one of the last income sources that an investor starting from scratch should look to set up. The exception to this is with Real Estate Investment Trusts (REITs). These are a type of mutual fund that allows investors to easily invest in actively managed real estate portfolios. There is more on these in chapter three.

Royalty income

Royalty income is income you make from licencing something you have created. This can be the use of patents, music, books or franchises. If you wrote a book or a song and sold it through an online store, you can earn royalty income from this. With royalty income, you put work and effort in at the start to create something and then you can earn royalties from what you create every time someone buys or uses your creation. In this way, it is active income at the start as you need to do work to create something. It then becomes passive as your creation is complete and the royalties come in with little or no further effort.

Whilst it can be easy to write off royalty income as something that would be hard to achieve, the rise of online book and music stores means earning royalty income is much more accessible for everyone. Everyone has an idea that they think could earn a million dollars. If more people spent the time to develop their ideas, they would surely eventually create something that could earn them some form of royalties. The potential to earn large sums of money over a long period of time is well within reach of anyone who is willing to put some time and effort into creating something of value. Similarly to every other form of income, the more thought and effort you put into creating the income stream, the more likely you are to be successful. And yes, just like the other income sources, royalty income is taxable.

Seven streams of income summary

 Earned income from job

 Capital Gains assets increased in value

 Profit income from buying and selling

 Dividend income from owning stocks

 Rental income from renting properties

 Royalty income from your IP / idea

 Interest income from lending

What the **f*ck** is investing?

Chapter 3:
Investing basics

What is an investor?

There are many players in the game of investing; retail investors are small fish in comparison to some of the other players in the market. You need to understand your place in the financial system to give yourself every chance of being successful. The question "What is an investor?" looks simple enough to answer on the surface but there are many different investors with different motivations to be aware of.

Most investors fall under one of three categories; retail investors, speculators and institutions. You should be very clear which type of investor you are. A lot of people lose money because they speculate when they think they're investing and vice versa. I see lots of statistics claiming that a majority of retail investors lose money in the stock market. Who knows what the actual figure is but you shouldn't really care. You just don't want to be one of them. By knowing when you risk moving from investing to speculating, you lower your risk of making poor decisions.

Retail Investor

A retail investor is a non-professional who buys an asset based on their research of its fundamental value or future value. You will also see this type of investor being referred to as a retail investor. This is the category of investor you and I both fall under. Retail investors come under a lot of criticism from professional investors and they will say that they lack the discipline, knowledge and expertise to properly research their investments. This is exactly what we want to change, as retail investors we should strive to develop the discipline, knowledge and expertise that will make us successful.

In January 2021, retail investors proved they can be a very influential group. An organised group of retail investors from an online forum called WallStreetBets hit headlines in January 2021. They managed to move the price per share of a company called GameStop from around $5 to over $350 in the space of a few days. Of course, the share price crashed back down again soon after, no doubt leaving a lot of investors at a massive loss. Whilst this was happening, all this caused institutions that had bet against GameStop shares to lose billions of dollars. This also caused wider market sell offs as institutional investors sold shares to raise cash and weather any further market upsets.

Technically anyone who pays into a pension is a retail investor but in the case of a pension, you usually don't have a huge amount of influence over what investments your pension buys unless you have a self-invested pension. Retail investors should read balance sheets, annual statements, regulatory news releases and wider news that could affect the stock. Retail investors should invest over a longer period of at least 3-5 years. For each retail investor, their risk tolerance and their return targets will be different and so different investments will appeal to different retail investors.

Most of this book focusses on retail investors. That is not to say you shouldn't understand how other categories of investors work though. You can gain valuable insights by

What the **f*ck** is investing?

looking at what speculators and institutions are doing. Money invested by institutions is sometimes referred to as "smart money". This is because institutions have professional investors working for them who spend years studying markets. Looking at institutions and speculators will help you spot opportunities where "smart money" is going and therefore improve your investment decisions.

Speculator

Speculators buy an asset because they believe it will increase in price. Speculators are also known as high frequency traders or day traders. Day traders don't believe prices will move based on the fundamentals of the asset but usually the belief is driven by market news, world events or technical analysis of price charts. Technical analysis involves looking closely at reoccurring trends in historical price data. The underlying assumption with this type of trading is that past price changes can be an indicator of future price changes.

Speculators have no real interest in the asset they are buying and a good speculator will usually have target buy and sell prices to prevent large losses or to try and take profit where they believe the peak of a price movement is. A common mistake retail investors often make is trading frequently, speculating and becoming a day trader, often losing money as a result.

Whilst there is no problem being either a speculator or an investor, it is important that a person does not try to do both with the same asset. When a speculator holds onto a stock past their previously set price targets, they become an investor. When an investor buys a stock without looking at the stocks fundamentals, they become a speculator. Both situations are dangerous and should be avoided.

Institutional investor

An institutional investor is an organisation that invests on behalf of other people. These include organisations such as banks, insurance companies and pension funds. These organisations usually have substantial capital to invest and so have the ability to hire experts. These experts have the time, training and discipline to find what they consider to be the best investments for the clients or customers.

The substantial capital that institutions employ can have the ability to influence financial markets. An institution buying or selling a large position in a stock can influence the stock price. For example, if a fund decided to buy $5 million worth of stock in a company currently valued at $100 million, this buy would represent 5% of that company and would likely move the stock price upwards. The opposite is also true, if it were to sell a large position, the stock price would likely fall.

This is where research is very important for retail investors. Knowing how much of a stock is held by institutions will give an insight into how volatile a stock is likely to be. A high proportion of institutional ownership tends to suggest a higher proportion of long term investors that are less likely to overreact to changing market conditions.

Some retail investors also base their investment decisions on what institutions are doing. Finding institutions with good analysts, finding what assets they are buying and then copying can make a successful strategy. The problem with this however is that if you do not research the fundamentals, you are not investing, you are speculating. Knowing what institutions are up to is just one tool in the retail investors' research toolbox. We will look in detail at these tools in chapter four.

The power of compounding

One of the most basic yet powerful investing principles is often overlooked by new investors; the power of compounding. Compounding is when your investments earn a return which is then reinvested. You then earn a return on your returns as well as your original investment. This has the effect of exponentially increasing your investment over time.

There are three things that influence the compounding of your investment; time, return rate and taxes/fees. The higher your return rate or longer the time invested, the higher its value will become. Taxes and fees have the opposite effect. The higher your taxes or fees, the less its value will become. It is easy to overlook a small fee on an investment but it is important to remember that fees can compound in the same way as interest. When small fees compound over a long period of time, fees can cost you a lot of money.

Where possible, minimise fees and taxes by using tax efficient accounts if they are available and low or zero fee investments. It should already be obvious that we want to maximise our rate of return where possible but it is sometimes less obvious how important the time element is. If you are lucky enough to have time on your side, you have much more capacity to grow your investments than someone who does not have time on their side. As Warren Buffet famously said; "It's not timing the market that's important, its time in the market."

Types of investment

There are many types of investment, each with their advantages and disadvantages. Some of the investments below such as mutual funds, stocks and commodities can be traded on stock exchanges. A stock exchange is a mechanism that matches buyers with sellers to allow them to trade. There are many stock exchanges in the world and you are not limited to only investing in your local exchange. Most brokers will allow investors to trade on a wide number of exchanges based in different countries. Investors will choose the different investment types below based on their investment goals and their attitude to risk.

Real estate

Real estate is a term that covers property, buildings, land and any rights attached to it. There are four categories of real estate that you can invest in; residential, commercial, industrial and land. Residential real estate is homes or property where people can live. Commercial real estate is real estate used for business purposes including offices, hotels and shopping centres. Industrial real estate is used in the manufacture or distribution of goods and includes factories and warehouses. Land real estate can be any land and is usually split into land that has been developed in the past (brownfield) and land that has never been developed (greenfield).

There are a few ways you can invest in real estate. You could either buy whole properties from the categories above or you could invest in a Real Estate Investment Trust (REIT). A REIT is a type of collective fund that only invests in real estate. Investing in a REIT has the advantage of requiring less capital but then also carries the same risk as investing in any fund; you're relying on the good management of the fund by its managers.

Buying whole properties will require a large amount of capital and then work to add value to the property. Buying an entire property will also require debt if you don't have the capital to make the purchase yourself. Debt means paying

What the **f*ck** is investing?

interest and paying interest means less returns. Dealing with tenants and the risk of tenants defaulting or damaging your property are risks involved with buying and letting properties.

Real estate generally goes up in value in economic climates where interest rates are low. This is because the cost of debt is lower and encourages people to buy homes, increasing demand and pushing prices higher. In contrast, in times of high interest rates, more people default on mortgages debt is harder to get and so demand for housing goes down therefore driving prices down.

Bonds & Certificates of Deposit

Bonds and certificates of deposit are offered by most banks and financial institutions. They offer the investor a fixed rate of return in exchange for leaving their money in an account for a fixed period of time, usually several years. Bonds tend to be longer term than certificates of deposit. You can think of a bond or certificate of deposit as you lending your money to a financial institution for a fixed period of time. In return they promise to pay you a fixed interest rate every year and promise to return your money after an agreed period of time.

You could go to a bank for example and purchase a bond for $1000 that matures in 5 years and promises to pay an interest rate of 3% per year. This means the bank will pay you $30 per year for 5 years. After 5 years it will also return your $1000. In total, for lending your $1000 to the bank for 5 years in this case, you would receive $30 * 5 = $150 in interest.

This type of bond is considered among the low risk investment types but along with their lower risk often comes lower rewards. They tend to be perceived as lower risk as the chances of major financial institutions or governments going bust and not repaying your money is considered to be low. There are still risks involved with bonds though; the financial institution you buy a bond from could default and never pay your money back.

At the time of writing, with record low interest rates, the return rates are less than 0.5% for certificates of deposit. This means that inflation is highly likely to reduce the value of your investment. Remember, if inflation rates are higher than interest rates, your money is losing value in a savings account.

It is also possible to invest in corporate bonds, offered by corporations as an inexpensive way of them raising cash. These often offer better rates than bonds from banks but also carry more risk. The risk is higher because you are relying on the financial stability of the company that issued the bond. Governments also offer bonds called Gilts which you can invest in, these are regarded as relatively safe investments depending on the government that issued them. It is considered very unlikely for example that the United States government will go bankrupt therefore bonds issued by them are seen as safe investments. Bonds can be traded and issued on the bond market in a similar way to stocks and shares on the stock market.

Bonds are a good investment in times of economic uncertainty because of their low risk. When interest rates are low, bond prices tend to increase as investors seek better returns. When interest rates rise, bond prices drop as the risk-reward becomes less attractive for investors.

Stocks and shares

A share is part ownership of a company listed on a stock exchange. When you buy shares in a company, you are buying a part of that company and the right to the future earnings of the company in proportion to your ownership. The term stock can be used interchangeably with shares. The only difference is that the term stock refers to the ownership of many companies whereas shares refer to the ownership of a specific company.

The main reason companies list shares on stock exchanges is to raise capital to invest back into their business and then grow. These shares are then traded between investors on stock exchanges. Buying shares is inherently risky, especially if you are inexperienced. Share prices can be volatile and there is a risk that inexperienced investors can invest in overpriced shares which then lose value.

Consider an example where a company issues 100 shares, where the 100 shares represent 100% ownership of the company. If the shares sell for £10 each, the company's total value or "market capitalisation" will be 10 * 100 = £1000. If you were to buy 10 shares in this company, you would own 10% of that company. The value of these shares can go up or down based on the company's performance and how people feel about the company's potential.

If the company released favourable financial results, the share price might rise to £11 per share for example. If you sold your 10 shares at this price, you would receive £110, making a profit of £10. In contrast, if the company released unfavourable results, the opposite could happen. The shares might then trade for £9 per share. If you sold your 10 shares then you would receive £90, making a loss of £10 in the process. You can see how this is one of the risks with stock market investing. There are a lot of things that can influence the price a company's shares trade for. Financial performance is one of the biggest factors and that is why we do research before we buy shares.

Another risk when investing in shares is called dilution. A company might decide it needs to raise funds and one way it can do this is by issuing more shares. When a company does this, your ownership of the company is reduced or "diluted". Using the same example as before, if the same company issues another 100 shares, the total number of shares outstanding would now be 200. You still own 10 shares except that now your 10 shares represent 5% ownership instead of 10%.

With the extra risk in stocks, comes potential for greater rewards. If you own shares in a company and the company goes bankrupt, you could lose your entire investment. Similarly, if you invested in a company and their share price doubled, you would double your investment. This is why research is very important before investing in stocks. The more research you do, the more likely you are to find the company that goes up in value instead of down.

Commodities

Commodities are physical materials or goods that are mined or produced. Oil, copper, wheat and livestock are all examples of commodities. They are the raw materials our economies are built upon. Without these goods, our economies could not function. We could not produce homes, energy or anything else we rely upon day to day.

Commodity prices are commonly influenced by world events and political news. Commodities can be traded like stocks and shares on exchanges. Commodities are traded by investors who use them to mitigate the risk of inflation. This is due to the link between commodities and the goods they are made from.

Commodities are used to produce those goods and services. When the demand for goods and services increases,

What the **f*ck** is investing?

commodity prices increase. They are also traded by speculators who trade them to take advantage of their volatility. Depending on the commodity, commodity investing can be risky. Commodity prices often fluctuate by up to 30% on any given day. In comparison, currencies prices tend to fluctuate by up to 10% on any given day.

Commodity prices tend to be more volatile because the supply cannot be changed quickly to meet either short term rises or falls in demand. Consider the 2020 pandemic and oil prices. Almost overnight the demand for oil crashed due to the drastic downturn in global aviation and transport as countries locked down their borders. This led to an oversupply of oil and therefore a drop in prices.

Mutual funds

You can think of a mutual fund as a collection of securities or assets. A mutual fund can hold stocks, commodities or bonds. Often, they will track an index such as the UK stock market. In the case of a mutual fund that tracks the UK stock market, the fund will own shares in every company in that market. It will own shares in proportion to each company's weighting in the index. In short it means that a fund that tracks an index will go up when the companies in the index go up and down when the companies in the index go down. You can think of it as investing in many companies and not just one. This way it spreads the risk of investing across many companies. This type of mutual fund also tends to be passively managed and as such they tend to incur low fees.

Some types of fund can be traded like stocks so they offer a convenient and easy way to invest in large groups of securities. Most retail investors couldn't invest easily in oil or livestock for example. Some specialised mutual funds offer the opportunity to invest in commodities like this without actually having to handle the underlying asset.

Mutual funds sometimes offer less risk than investing in individual stocks or securities as the risk is spread across more assets. As with all investments, it is good to research mutual funds before investing. Specialised mutual funds might offer more risk than funds tracking large indexes for example. The main reason for this is that they are less diversified than a fund that has a wider range of assets.

To illustrate why diversification is important, imagine that in January 2020 a fund was set up that invested solely in the aviation industry. It bought shares in airlines, airplane manufacturers and oil companies. Now fast forward three months when countries started locking down their borders and airlines stopped flying. Stock prices of airlines, airplane manufacturers and oil companies all crashed. Imagine how much less that fund would be worth in that situation than a fund that tracked a major index like the FTSE 100. The major index fund would still be down in value but nowhere near as much as the airline fund.

A key part to consider when looking at funds is that some of them are actively managed. Actively managed just means there is a person that manages the fund and where the fund invests. The quality of this management can vary greatly and also the fees they charge for the privilege can vary greatly. Remember not to overlook the importance of fees; these can have a huge impact on your overall investment over the long term. In chapter six you will see an example demonstrating how fees can affect your investment.

The mutual fund type that is most useful to us as retail investors is the Exchange traded fund (ETF). ETFs have a mechanism that will ensure the overall trading price of shares in the fund is close to the funds' net asset value. In other words, when more money comes into the fund from investors, more shares in its underlying assets are bought. When money is demanded from the fund, shares in the underlying assets are sold. This happens automatically to make the overall value of the fund equal to the value of the assets it holds.

There are hundreds of ETFs available for retail investors to invest in. This is one of the huge benefits of ETFs; there is so much choice that you can find a fund for almost every investor. They can be traded just like shares through most brokers and so they are incredibly easy to invest in. ETFs can take the risk away from picking individual stocks and so are ideal for investors who aren't confident in stock picking. You can buy both actively and passively managed ETFs that specialise in nearly every industry. You can also find ETFs that track whole indexes or even some that track more than one index. ETFs are a great starting point for anyone new to investing.

ETFs should not be confused with Exchange traded notes (ETNs). An ETN is a form of debt issued by a financial institution. They track an index of some sort and promise to pay the investor the value of the index after an agreed period of time minus a management fee. Because ETNs do not hold an underlying asset such as shares or commodities, they present an extra level of risk. You are essentially relying upon the credit worthiness of the bank that issued the ETN. If institution that issued the ETN went bust, there would be no assets held in the ETN from which to pay back investors.

They have tax advantages in certain regions over ETFs and they track indexes much more accurately. Look at what happened to banks during the 2008 financial crisis and then decide whether you think these are good investments. I'll give you a hint; a lot of banks went bust. The moral of the story is when investing in a mutual fund, make sure you are aware of what type of fund it is and what the assets it holds are. ETFs are popular with retail investors as they are easily tradable, easy to understand and there are huge selections available. If you think mutual funds are for you, the first place I suggest you start is with ETFs.

Gold

Gold is considered a hybrid commodity in that it is both a currency and a commodity. It deserves a mention of its own as it is one of the oldest types of investment. Humans have attributed value to gold for thousands of years because of its scarcity and physical properties. The scarcity of gold is important as this means there is almost a fixed amount of it in the market. There is very little risk of a supplier suddenly flooding the market with gold as happens with other commodities such as oil.

Gold is an unreactive metal and as such it does not tarnish and is therefore attractive in appearance. This is why it has been used to produce items of value such as coins and jewellery for thousands of years. Until this century, most currencies were backed up by physical gold. If a currency is backed by gold it just means that each unit of the currency has a set amount of gold stored in a vault that it is backed up by. Although most currencies are no longer backed by the "gold standard" any more, most people still believe gold has value.

Gold is seen as a good way to mitigate or "hedge" against inflation. Whilst the supply of currencies and goods tends to go up and therefore inflation with it, the supply of gold is very limited and so it holds its value. Over a long period of time, gold is seen as a relatively low risk investment. Gold is considered lower risk because its relatively fixed supply means the value of gold tends to rise. Like other commodities and currencies, it can experience short term volatility and so that should be considered before investing.

There are several ways of investing in gold. The first is to physically buy gold. You can buy physical gold as an investment in the form of coins and bullion bars. In most countries, you can buy gold in this way tax free; however check the rules where you live to be sure. The second and third ways to invest in gold are through exchange traded funds and exchange traded notes (see mutual funds). All three methods have their advantages and disadvantages.

Buying physical gold and taking delivery of it has the benefit of your own control; you have the asset in your hand and can control what you do with it. This has obvious security risks though as I doubt your house has its own vault. If you opt not to take delivery and instead store it in a vault, you will have to pay fees for that privilege. Another drawback is the large spreads you will encounter when buying physical gold. The spread means you have to pay a higher price for the gold than you could get if you sold it straight away. Therefore as soon as you buy it, you have technically made a loss until the gold price rises above the price you paid for it.

When buying gold through ETFs and ETNs, you might have fees to pay both in the management of the fund and the storage of the gold. ETNs also have the disadvantage of not actually owning any gold so you are investing in the credit worthiness of the underwriter of the ETN. In my book, that is a big mark against gold ETNs.

Foreign exchange

Currencies can be traded on the foreign exchange market 24 hours a day. This is a mechanism to convert one currency to another. I would argue that investing in currencies on the foreign exchange market is inherently speculative in a similar way to investing in certain commodities. As private investors, you should aim to avoid speculative investments.

One less speculative way to invest in currencies is through mutual funds and shares held in other countries. When those assets produce returns, the returns can be in a different currency than your home currency. The fluctuations in value between those two currencies can then either boost or reduce your returns. For example, if you invested in a company listed on the Australian stock exchange, it would pay any returns in Australian dollars. If you lived in the USA, you would have to convert those Australian dollars to US dollars. If the US dollar gained value against the Australian dollar, you returns would be reduced. If the US dollar lost value, your gains would be increased.

Cryptocurrencies

Cryptocurrencies are a relatively new type of investment. They were invented as a way of transferring value i.e. a currency. Recently however, people having been using cryptocurrencies to store value. The suitability of cryptocurrencies as an investment is subject to much debate. I would argue that they are inherently speculative and therefore not an investment. There are many fraudulent cryptocurrencies created to take money from inexperienced investors. The lack of regulation in the industry and often the threat of more regulation make investing in cryptocurrencies a bit of a lottery.

What the **f*ck** is investing?

Cryptocurrency exchanges are also notorious targets for hackers who in the past have been successful in stealing digital assets from investors without them being able to do anything about it. Security is a big issue when investing in cryptocurrencies. Buying cryptocurrencies is probably the riskiest and most volatile way of investing money. If you are new to investing or you don't want to lose money, you should stay clear of cryptocurrencies.

If you do decide to buy cryptocurrencies, make sure the broker you are using is reputable and that you maintain good online security habits such as strong unique passwords and two factor authentication. As with any investment, remember that you can lose your entire investment. Again, if you intend on investing in this area, make sure you do your research and understand what it is you are buying. If you don't understand the investment, you are not investing, you are speculating.

Annuities and life insurance

An annuity is a financial product that pays out a fixed income to a person until they die. The person pays a sum of money to a financial institution and is guaranteed a certain income in return. The person is guaranteed that no matter what happens to interest rates or financial markets, they will still get their fixed income. The financial organisation continues paying this fixed income until the person dies. This presents a risk to the institution as the longer the person lives, the more money the annuity will cost them. If the person outlives their initial investment, the financial institution will have lost money.

As an example, imagine at the age of 65 you paid £100,000 for an annuity of £5000 per year. This means that you would need to live to 85 to break even on that investment assuming you don't include inflation (£5000 * 20 years= £100,000). If you don't live until you're 85, you would have been paid less than the £100,000 you originally invested; the financial institution makes a gain. If you live past 85, it means the financial institution will have to pay more than your original investment; in other words, you make a gain.

These financial institutions often hedge against this risk by also issuing life insurance policies. Life insurance policies pay out in the event of an investors' death. The investor will pay a fixed amount of money per month to the financial institution for the policy until they die. If the person dies prematurely, the institution will have to pay out more money than they received from the investor, making a net loss in the process. On the other hand, the investor could also live beyond the period expected, meaning the financial institution will make a net gain.

Take another example. Suppose at the age of 65, you take out a life insurance policy that will pay out £100,000 in the event of your death. The insurance company charges you £5000 per year for this policy. If you die in the next 20 years, the insurance company in this case will have to pay out more than you paid in. If you live longer than 20 years, you will have paid more than what your policy is worth and so the insurance company will have made a gain.

You can see how annuities and life insurance policies are natural hedges against each other. One deals with the risk of longevity and the other with the risk of dying prematurely. In most countries, you can't actually purchase an annuity until you are 55.

As a result, they are often used by retirees to secure an income in their retirement when they are unwilling or unable to work. Annuities are not recommended investments for younger people as they often have financial penalties for withdrawing money prematurely.

Life insurance investment is very much down to the individual, for obvious reasons, the individual will never actually be able to profit from the investment themselves. Instead, life insurance is designed to protect financial dependants in the case of a persons' death.

Chapter 4:
Valuing **investments**

I've said a few times already but I can't overstate how important it is; research. The foundation of stock research is learning how to estimate the value of a company. Valuing a company might seem like a daunting task but it really isn't if you use the right tools. You don't need to create complicated spreadsheets or use scientific calculators to get these valuations. There are much easier and more accessible ways of doing it. The most important thing is to learn to cut through the jargon and get to the numbers and news events that influence a company's value. This chapter will explain what you need to know and where to find it. It will also show you how to take the numbers and produce valuations without having to do any calculations by hand.

Where to find information

When researching your investments, you should ensure your information sources are reliable. There are a growing number of private investors that buy investments based on reading so called "facts" on internet forums and social media. The problem is that on most websites, there is no regulation and people can say whatever they want whether it is true or not.

In my time spent reading internet forums, it became clear to me how much misinformation is spread on the internet about investments. I've seen examples of so called stock tippers sharing information on twitter, the share price of their stock then spikes upwards as naïve investors pile in. The next thing that happens is that share price collapses leaving those investors at a loss. It doesn't take a detective to guess who the person was that sold the stock first when the price spiked. This tactic is called "pump and dump" and it is something to be wary of. Don't get drawn into speculation and hysteria around investments. Stick to solid facts only.

Always independently verify any information you read online. Assume that anyone discussing shares online is trying to deceive you and you will be much less likely to make a mistake. If you come across any experts promoting companies, research that person before you do anything. Often searching the persons' name on a search engine will give you an idea of their motivation. I've seen examples of influencers promoting shares on twitter. I've then searched online to find out the so called influencer has been involved in bad business deals and countless bankrupt companies. Not all company directors have their shareholders best interests at heart. The Alternative Investment Market (AIM) in the UK at a time was known as the wild west of investing and was notorious for private investors losing money because of its relatively lax regulation.

Trustworthy information sources online are few and far between, this is why scepticism is healthy when investing. You wouldn't give thousands of your hard earned cash to a random guy on the street that you don't know would you? Why give it to a random company that you don't know anything about just because your mate on twitter said it was definitely going to go up in value?

What the **f*ck** is investing?

Good information is information you can independently verify elsewhere. Regulated sources are good to use. News and market releases made by legitimate companies are a good source of research. Remember that the more mature and regulated the market where the company is listed, the more you should be able to rely on the quality of information released by companies. Often the broker you use will have research resources you can use for free.

First party sources such as the websites of the companies themselves as well as the websites of the stock exchanges that list companies are the most accurate and reliable sources of information. For example, the FTSE 100 website holds all the regulatory news released made by companies listed on the FTSE 100. Sources like this are great in terms of their reliability. Through these sources you should be able to access financial statements, news releases, share price information and other trustworthy news sources.

How to value a company

In order to decide what investments are likely to give you a return on your money, you have to estimate what their current or future value is. This allows you to buy investments that are more likely to be undervalued and so have the highest probability of increasing in value. There is more than one way of valuing a business and as such, there is much debate over what the best method is. There are so many ways of doing it that it can be quite daunting at first. The good news is that the internet makes doing this much more accessible for private investors. For some of the methods below, www.wtfinvesting.com has free calculators you can use. Remember, if you are not sure of something, there is always a resource online that can help. All of the figures you need to value a company should be included in its latest financial statement.

What's in a financial statement?

Reading financial statements is something you have to do as part of your investment research. If you don't know how to read a financial statement, you shouldn't be picking your own stocks. It is simply too risky. Companies will usually release financial statements within their annual report, some companies report more often. Annual reports are a treasure trove of useful information for investors. Often they contain droves of information such as the company's structure, their executives' pay and their future plans. There are three main tables within a financial statement that are the most useful to use when valuing a company. These are the income statement, cash flow statement and the balance sheet.

At first glance they can seem like a complicated mass of numbers but you just need to know what the terms mean. In this chapter is an example of an income statement, cash flow statement and a balance sheet. All the terms you need to know are then explained and at the end of the chapter, I've even summarised the key terms in a handy table for you to refer back to.

Income statement

An income statement summarises all the company's finances for the period covered. It will show how profitable a company was over the reporting period; some companies release income statements quarterly and some annually. Income statements are sometimes referred to as "net income statements", "statement of earnings" or "profit and loss statement". An example income statement is below. I will refer back to this sheet later in the chapter:

Income statement example

	Note	2020 US$m	2019 US$m
Revenue	5(a)	3,922	3,742
Cost of sales	5(b)	(2,568)	(2,648)
Gross profit		1,354	1,094
Exploration expenses	11	(64)	(70)
Corporate administration expenses	5(c)	(117)	(120)
Other income/(expenses)	5(d)	55	38
Share of profit/(loss) of associates	31	(37)	(18)
Write-down of property, plant and equipment	6	(20)	–
Major transaction and integration costs	6	(15)	–
Profit before interest and income tax		1,156	924
Finance income		19	26
Finance costs	5(e)	(190)	(120)
Net finance costs		(171)	(94)
Profit before income tax		985	830
Income tax expense	7(a)	(350)	(272)
Profit after income tax		635	558
Profit after tax attributable to:			
Non-controlling interests		(12)	(3)
Owners of the parent		647	561
		635	558
Earnings per share (cents per share)			
Basic earnings per share	8	83.4	73.0
Diluted earnings per share	8	83.1	72.8

Cash flow statement

A cash flow statement summarises a company's' incoming and outgoing cash flows over a reporting period. The cash flow statement allows investors to understand how well the company is managing its operations. The main difference between the cash flow statement and the income statement is that the cash flow statement shows the actual money that went through the company in that period. The income statement on the other hand, might include expected income or expenses that might not have been paid yet. An example cash flow statement is below. I will refer back to this sheet later in the chapter:

Cash flow statement example

US$m	2020	2019	Change	Change %
Cash flow from operating activities[4]	1,471	1,487	(16)	(1%)
Production stripping and sustaining capital expenditure	(422)	(378)	(44)	(12%)
Major capital expenditure	(273)	(153)	(120)	(78%)
Total capital expenditure	(695)	(531)	(164)	(31%)
Reclassification of capital leases[4]	4	-	4	
Exploration and evaluation expenditure	(113)	(78)	(35)	(45%)
Receipts from Fruta del Norte finance facilities[10]	1	-	1	
Proceeds from sale of property, plant and equipment	2	-	2	
Free cash flow (before M&A activity)[3]	**670**	**878**	**(208)**	**(24%)**
Acquisition payment for a 70% interest of Red Chris[9]	(769)	-	(769)	
Acquisition of Fruta del Norte finance facilities[10]	(460)	-	(460)	
Payment for investment in Lundin Gold	(79)	(10)	(69)	(690%)
Payment for investment in SolGold	-	(18)	18	100%
Proceeds from sale of Gosowong, net of cash divested[8]	20	-	20	
Proceeds from sale of Séguéla	-	20	(20)	(100%)
Payments for other investments	(3)	(66)	63	95%
Free cash flow	**(621)**	**804**	**(1,425)**	**(177%)**

Balance sheet

A balance sheet shows the value of all assets and liabilities that the company holds or owes. The difference between the assets and liabilities is called the shareholder equity. The assets, liabilities and shareholder equity should always balance, hence the name balance sheet.

You can check this on the balance sheet below. The total assets are $13,242 million and the total liabilities are $4629 million. If you subtract $4,629 million from $13,242 million, you will see that it is equal to $8,613 million. In other words, it is equal to the shareholder equity as shown on the balance sheet below.

What the f*ck is investing?

Balance sheet example

US$m	As at 30 June			
	2020	2019	Change	Change %
Assets				
Cash and cash equivalents	1,451	1,600	(149)	(9%)
Trade and other receivables	305	135	170	126%
Inventories	1,573	1,573	-	0%
Other financial assets	546	103	443	430%
Current tax asset	1	32	(31)	(97%)
Property, plant and equipment	8,809	7,816	993	13%
Goodwill	17	-	17	
Other intangible assets	24	33	(9)	(27%)
Deferred tax assets	65	60	5	8%
Investment in associates	386	333	53	16%
Other assets	65	152	(87)	(57%)
Total assets	**13,242**	**11,837**	**1,405**	**12%**
Liabilities				
Trade and other payables	(520)	(444)	(76)	(17%)
Current tax liability	(23)	(176)	153	87%
Borrowings	(2,017)	(1,995)	(22)	(1%)
Other financial liabilities	(274)	(123)	(151)	(123%)
Provisions	(623)	(524)	(99)	(19%)
Lease liabilities⁴	(58)	-	(58)	
Deferred tax liabilities	(1,114)	(944)	(170)	(18%)
Total liabilities	**(4,629)**	**(4,206)**	**(423)**	**(10%)**
Net assets	**8,613**	**7,631**	**982**	**13%**
Equity				
Equity attributable to owners of the parent	8,613	7,567	1,046	14%
Non-controlling interests	-	64	(64)	(100%)
Total equity	**8,613**	**7,631**	**982**	**13%**

A company's assets are all the things of value that a company owns, creates or benefits from. Assets can include a large number of things from cash to land or machinery. A company's total liabilities are all the combined debt a company owes. Taxes, salaries and loans to be paid are all examples of liabilities.

Balance sheets allow investors to see how much cash or debt the company has and how efficient its operations are. I will refer back to the balance sheet above later in the chapter:

What terms do I need to know?

The following terms are usual to know and can be read straight from the financial statements or easily calculated from figures on the financial statement.

Revenue

Revenue is the total income generated from all of the company's activities before costs are deducted. Revenue may also be referred to as the top line, sales or turnover. Revenue only takes into account a company's ability to make sales as it doesn't include the cost of those sales. It is one of the first numbers to look for when viewing a financial statement. Comparing a company's revenue from year to year can give an investor an idea of whether the company is growing or shrinking. Revenue can be found at the top of the income statement.

Profit

Profit is the revenue minus any costs required to generate that revenue. Profit may also be referred to as earnings, income or net income. Comparing the revenue to the profit gives an investor an idea of the quality of the company. The higher the profit in proportion to its revenue the more efficient and cost effective a company is.

Some companies also include other measures of profit on their income statements. An example is earnings before tax interest (EBIT), otherwise known as operating profit. The point of a measure like this is to remove factors that a company has discretion over such as debt, depreciation and taxes to put the profit figure in a different perspective.

If you compare a company's profits and costs year to year, you can get an idea of whether the company is becoming more efficient. As investors you want to see a company reduce its costs year to year but increase its revenue and profit. Profit can be found on the income statement.

Return on sales

The return on sales is the operating profit divided by the net sales or revenue. An increasing return on sales year to year indicates a company is becoming more efficient at managing its costs. A decreasing return on sales year to year might indicate that a company is losing control of its costs. Return on sales can be calculated from figures found on the income statement.

Net asset value (NAV)

A company's NAV is its total assets minus its total liabilities. Both figures should be available on the balance sheet. The NAV is in principle what the company would be worth if the company was liquidated. To calculate the NAV per share, divide the NAV by the total number of shares. The NAV is found on the balance sheet and the total number of shares on the annual report.

Return on equity

The return on equity is a measure of how efficiently a company has generated its profits. The return on equity may also be referred to as the return on assets. The return on equity is the company's' profits divided by its net assets. The return on equity gives investors another tool to compare the performance of a company against other similar companies. If a company has a higher return on equity than its peers, its potential for growth is usually considered to be higher. However, the down side of this is if a company's return on equity is much higher than its peers, its growth may not be sustainable. Investors should look for a return on equity that is higher than the market average. The market average for the S&P500 is 14% so for an S&P 500 company, you would want to look at companies with a return on equity that is higher than 14%. The return on equity can be calculated using figures from the income statement and the balance sheet.

Retention ratio

Retention ratio is the amount of profit a company retains in order to reinvest in itself. It is calculated by dividing the retained profit by the total profit. When used along with the return on equity for a company, it can give an idea of how sustainable a company's growth is. The retention ratio will also give investors an idea of whether the company is likely to grow. A company that pays out 100% of its profits has not left any money to invest in itself and would be less likely to grow as a result. The retained profit can be found on a company's annual report and the profit on its income statement.

Sustainable growth rate

When you multiply the retention ratio and the return on equity, you get what is called the sustainable growth rate. This is the maximum rate that company will be able to grow without borrowing money. If a company's growth rate is higher than its' sustainable growth rate, the company will not be able to maintain that rate of growth without raising more money. If the growth rate is less than the sustainable growth rate, the company has more capacity to grow than it is currently doing. This is one way an investor can decide on the likelihood that a company is going to grow in the coming years and how any growth might impact an investment. The sustainable growth rate can be calculated using figures from the balance sheet, income statement and annual report.

What the **f*ck** is investing?

Price to book ratio (P/B)

The price to book ratio is a comparison of the value of a company's total assets to its market value. To get the P/B ratio, you just need to divide the current share price by the company's net asset value per share. A P/B ratio of one means that a company's market value and its total asset value are equal. If the P/B ratio is less than one, it indicates the company could be undervalued. The P/B ratio can be calculated using figures from the balance sheet and annual report.

Free cash flow

Free cash flow is found by deducting the cost of any capital expenditures from the company's cash flow figure. Capital expenditure is expenditure on any assets that improve the company's capacity or capabilities in some way.

Free cash flow gives an investor an idea of how much money the company has to pay out to its investors or creditors. A free cash flow that reduces year to year may indicate that a company is experiencing financial weakness. Because free cash flow is heavily influenced by capital expenditure, year to year it can change substantially. If a company invested in a lot of new equipment or offices in any given year, it could significantly reduce the free cash flow for that year. Free cash flow can be found on the cash flow statement.

Enterprise value

The enterprise value of a company is a useful metric as it allows you to spot companies that might be undervalued. The enterprise value takes into account debts and obligations which market capitalisation (the total value of all shares) does not. To calculate the enterprise value, you add the market capitalisation to its outstanding preferred stock and its debt. You then subtract any cash and cash equivalents held.

Price to earnings ratio (P/E)

Price to earnings ratio is a company's share price divided by its profits or earnings per share. It is a useful measure to use when comparing similar companies or a company to its own historical record. Price to earnings ratio may also be referred to as the price multiple or earnings multiple. As investors, we want to see low P/E ratios as they suggest the company is better value whereas a high P/E ratio suggests a company might be overvalued. This is why it is useful to use P/E ratio to compare similar companies in the same sector. Rather than using the P/E ratio as a standalone figure, you can compare it to similar companies in the sector to and make a better judgement on the value of the company at that time. P/E ratio can be calculated using values from the income statement.

Variation between income statements

Each of the terms above might appear differently on different income statements. If you look at two companies in the same industry yet listed in different countries, their statements will look very different at first glance but the information on each is usually the same.

They might have different terms for profit and revenue for example. The information you need might not be in the same section for different companies statements. Remember to consider the slightly different

What the **f*ck** is investing?

terminologies used from market to market. When reading an income statement, have the following table to hand to help you cut through the jargon and varying terminology. Keep referring back to the descriptions above too if you need to.

Financial metrics summary table

Measure	Also known as	Where to find	How its calculated
Revenue	Sales, top line, gross income	Income statement	Total sales
Profit	Earnings, income, net income	Income statement	$\frac{Revenue}{Total\ costs}$
EBITA		Income statement	$Net\ income + interest + taxes + amortisation$
EBIT	Operating profit	Income statement	$Net\ income + interest + taxes$
Retained profit		Income statement & annual report	$Total\ profit - total\ dividends$
Return on sales		Income statement	$\frac{Operating\ profit}{Revenue}$
Net assets	Net asset value (NAV)	Balance sheet	$Total\ assets - total\ liabilities$
Net asset value (NAV) per share		Balance sheet & annual report	$\frac{Net\ asset\ value}{Total\ shares}$
Earnings per share		Income statement & annual report	$\frac{Total\ profit}{Total\ shares}$
Return on equity	Return on assets, return on net assets	Income statement & balance sheet	$\frac{Profit}{Net\ assets}$
Retention ratio	Plowback ratio	Income statement & annual report	$\frac{Retained\ profit}{Total\ profit}$
Sustainable growth rate		Income statement, balance sheet & annual report	$Return\ on\ equity \times retention\ ratio$
Price to book (P/B) ratio		Balance sheet & annual report	$\frac{Share\ price}{NAV\ per\ share}$
Price to earnings (P/E) ratio	Price multiple, earnings multiple	Income statement	$\frac{Share\ price}{Earnings\ per\ share}$
Free cash flow		Cash flow statement	$\frac{Net\ cash\ flow}{Total\ capital\ expenditure}$
Enterprise value	Firm value, total enterprise value		$(All\ stock\ value + debt) - (Cash + Cash\ equivalents)$

Valuation methods

When you know what the figures mean on a financial statement, you now need to know how to apply those figures to work out a value for the company. We will look at three methods of valuing a company below. The first method is quick and easy but it will not be useful for every sector. The second method is more detailed but will consider more variables and therefore improve your valuation. The third method is the most comprehensive method and will give a much more accurate valuation.

Asset based valuation

An asset based valuation considers what a company would be worth if everything it owned was liquidated or sold. This method of valuation does not take into account the value of any income that could be generated from the company's assets and as such it is a fairly limited method to use. An asset based valuation method will be able to tell an investor if a company is undervalued but not if it is overvalued.

A lot of technology companies for example, do not own assets and yet they are extremely valuable companies. Uber and Air BnB are examples of this. This method is most useful for valuing commodity based companies such as mining companies.

The very first step in applying an asset based valuation is to look at the assets on its balance sheet. Work out the NAV per share. Compare this value to the current share price. If it is below the current share price, this indicates that the company may be undervalued.

This doesn't tell the whole story though. As I've said, not all assets are tangible or can be reported on a balance

What the **f*ck** is investing?

sheet. A gold mining company might have millions of tonnes of ore reserves worth billions of dollars that aren't reported on its balance sheet. A technology company might not have physical assets but might own billions of dollars of intellectual property. When using an asset based valuation, you should also read its annual report to get an understanding of any assets that have value but aren't reported on its balance sheet.

Asset valuation example

Now, let's run through this method on a mining company as an example. I picked a mining company at random, Newcrest Mining (NCM: ASX). It is their balance sheet, income statement and cash flow statement shown in the "What's in a financial statement" section.

In their case, you can see their net assets are $8,613 million US Dollars (USD). From Newcrest's annual report, I was able to find their total number of outstanding shares is approximately 778.5 million.

To get an asset value per share, divide the net assets by the outstanding shares:

$$Asset\ value\ per\ share = \frac{\$8,613\ million\ USD\ total\ assets}{778.5\ million\ total\ shares} = \$11.06\ USD$$

We need to compare this to the current share price of the company. The company is listed on the Australian stock exchange and so its share price is quoted in Australian dollars. The figures on its financial reports are in US dollars. We need to make sure we don't mix up currencies when doing a valuation like this.

Newcrest's share price at the time of writing was $27.28 Australian dollars (AUD). To convert this to USD, you multiply this number by the current exchange rate of 0.6715:

$$Share\ price\ in\ USD = \$27.28\ AUD * 0.6715\ (the\ exchange\ rate) = \$18.31\ USD$$

So does this mean the company is currently over valued? Possibly, however this number doesn't take into account any assets the company has in development and most importantly, it doesn't take into account any ore reserves the company already has. Let's add a value to the company's ore reserve too and then compare again.

In the same 2020 report, the company states that it has 52 million ounces of gold reserves alone. You can put a value on this as well. If we use their financial results summary shown above, you can see that the all in sustaining cost of their mining operations in 2020 were $862 USD per ounce of gold mined. The average price per ounce that they sold their gold for in 2020 was $1530 USD per ounce.

If you subtract the cost price of mining each ounce of gold from the sale price of each ounce of gold, you get the profit made for each ounce of gold mined:

$$Profit\ per\ ounce\ of\ gold\ mined = \$1530 - \$862 = \$668\ USD$$

Multiply this by the total gold reserve of 52 million ounces:

$$Value\ of\ gold\ reserve = 52\ million * \$668 = \$34,736\ million\ USD$$

What the f*ck is investing?

Add this to the net assets of $8,613:

$$\textit{Value of gold reserve and net assets} = \$34{,}736 \textit{ million} + \$8{,}613 \textit{ million}$$
$$= \$43{,}349 \textit{ million USD}$$

Now divide this number by the total number of shares:

$$\textit{Value per share of assets and gold reserves} = \frac{\$43{,}349 \textit{ million USD}}{778.5 \textit{ million total shares}}$$
$$= \$55.68 \textit{ USD}$$

Now compare that again to the current share price of $18.31 USD and it seems like a bargain, right? Well, not exactly. When we valued the ore reserves we valued them at a price we would get if we had them in our hand today. In reality it will take 20- 30 years to mine those reserves. This is where the discounted cash flow valuation method discussed later is useful.

The asset based valuation also doesn't take into account any revenue that can be generated from assets. It doesn't take into account the potential for the underlying asset prices to change (gold and copper in this case) or for future costs to rise either. So while this method could certainly tell us if a company is undervalued (if the per share asset price was less than the share price), more work is required to tell us if it is overvalued. This is why we must also use the next two methods, especially the discounted cash flow method to give us a better idea of the current value.

Comparable method

The next method we will look at considers more than just assets. It is a comparative approach as it will use average values for similar companies in its calculation. The underlying assumption with this type of method is that similar assets should sell for similar values. The first thing you need to do is to understand a bit about other companies in the same sector.

Comparable valuation methods simply compare the company directly to another company or the industry average. You can just compare their multiples and metrics directly. Comparing other metrics from the previous section such as assets, revenue, profits, growth rates and cash flows will also give an indication of whether company is undervalued in comparison to its peers.

If you apply this method, you will start to identify companies that are undervalued. The most undervalued ones are worth adding to a short list for a more in depth analysis using one of the methods that follow.

Comparable example

Consider again the example of Newcrest. Let's compare Newcrest to two similar companies, Newmont Corporation and Barrick Gold. A good way to do this is to calculate the comparable ratios for each company and put them in a table. Using the formulas from the financial metrics summary table shown previously, this is how to calculate Newcrest's comparable ratios:

To calculate Newcrest's P/E ratio, you can see from the income statement that their earnings per share figure was $0.834 USD. Divide the current share price of $18.31 USD by the earnings per share figure of $0.834 USD:

$$Price\ to\ earnings\ ratio = \frac{\$0.834\ (earnings\ per\ share)}{\$18.31\ (share\ price)} = 21.95$$

What the **f*ck** is investing?

Newcrest's enterprise value is calculated by first calculating the value of all its outstanding shares. This is the share price of $18.31USD multiplied by the total number of shares:

$$\$18.31 \ (share \ price) * 778.5 \ million \ shares = \$14,254 \ million \ USD$$

We now add the total value of Newcrest's debt of $2,017 million USD from the balance sheet above:

$$\$14,254 \ million + \$2,017 \ million = \$16,271 \ million \ USD$$

To find the enterprise value, we now subtract the value of all cash and cash equivalents of $1,451 million from the balance sheet:

$$Enterprise \ value = \ \$18,883 million - \$1,451 million = \$14,820 \ million \ USD$$

Now to find the free cash flow per share, we simply take the free cash flow figure from the cash flow statement of -$621 million USD and divide it by the total number of shares:

$$Free \ cash \ flow \ per \ share = \frac{-\$621 \ million}{778.5 \ million \ share} = -\$0.80 \ USD \ per \ share$$

We can now put these values in a table and compare to similar companies as shown below:

Company	Price (USD)	Enterprise value (million USD)	Revenue (million USD)	Earnings per share (USD)	Free cash flow per share (USD)	Enterprise value/ Revenue	Price/ Earnings
Newcrest	18.31	14,820	3,922	0.834	-0.8	3.78	21.95
Newmont	59.95	50,490	11,080	3.18	1.9	4.56	18.82
Barrick gold	22.54	60,000	12,200	1.7	1.52	5	17.04

From this table, you can see that Newcrest's P/E ratio is higher than the others and its earnings per share figure is also lower than the others. Its free cash flow is much lower than the others but this can be explained by significant acquisitions made in the reporting period. On the other hand, Newcrest has the lowest enterprise value to revenue ratio. When comparing Newcrest to its peers, the main concern is the low earnings in comparison to its peers. It would be worth examining the company further to see if there is an explanation for its lower earnings in comparison to its peers.

You can see how using a comparable valuation method can indicate both that a company might be overvalued but also that it might be undervalued. The comparable method is useful to check companies at a glance but you cannot get a solid valuation from this type of method. You can use it to immediately cross off companies with comparable metrics that are less favourable than others in their sector. To get a more solid valuation figure, let's try the third valuation method.

Discounted cash flow (DCF) analysis

The final method of determining the value of a company is by using a discounted cash flow analysis. The underlying assumption behind a DCF analysis is that money today is worth more than money in the future. Would you rather someone gave you £10,000 now or £100 per month over 100 months? Obviously you'd rather have the money now. A DCF analysis is just putting a value on future money expected to be received.

On the face of it, it can seem complicated to do yourself by hand but this is where the internet is your friend again. Calculating a DCF analysis by hand can lead to

What the **f*ck** is investing?

errors especially if you are not experienced in doing these calculations so at the start, I would definitely recommend making use of an online DCF calculator. Go to www. wtfinvesting.com to make use of the free DCF calculator there.

Now that you have a DCF calculator, you need to know what the numbers are that you need to input to the calculator.

The underlying formula for a DCF analysis is:

$$Discounted\ cash\ flow = \frac{Cash\ flow\ year\ 1}{1 + discount\ rate} + \frac{Cash\ flow\ year\ 2}{1 + discount\ rate} + \frac{Cash\ flow\ year\ n}{1 + discount\ rate}$$

Where n = number of years before cash flow occurs.

Again, don't worry if you don't know how to apply the formula, remember you have a calculator online that can do that bit for you. You just need to know what each number in the formula means. You can get the current years cash flow from the company's financial statement to get the first years cash flow.

In order to estimate cash flow for years to come, you need to estimate a growth rate for the company. Usually, the growth rate is broken into two rates: the short term rate and the long term rate. You can also think of the maximum long term rate as the sustainable growth rate discussed previously.

You can use the company's previous 5 year average growth rate as a guide for the short term rate. If the growth is increasing year to year, this will be a good guide. If it is reducing year to year, you should use a value that is less than the 5 year average.

Now you need to choose a discount rate. This is usually the return that you could get from another investment over the same period. Often the return from a benchmark index such as the S&P 500 is used.

Finally, you need to know either the cash flow or the earnings per share. If you use cash flow, you will need to divide the results of the calculation by the total number of shares to get a valuation per share. If you use the earnings per share figure, the result of the calculation will be the valuation per share. Now, all you need to do is plug those numbers into the calculator and you get a value for the company out.

DCF Example

So let's apply this technique to our example company, Newcrest.

First, we need our earnings per share figure. We have already calculated this to be $0.834 USD.

We now need to estimate a growth rate for the company. Between 2019 and 2020, its profits grew 15% and by looking back at previous statements, its five year average growth rate is 13.6%. Let's assume a growth rate of 13.6% for the next 5 years and then use the sustainable growth rate as the long term growth rate.

Let's now assume the long term growth rate is equal to the sustainable growth rate. To calculate the sustainable growth rate we first need to find its retention ratio. Looking at its last annual report, Newcrest paid $0.25 USD per share dividends and earned $0.834 USD per share. The retained profit per share is:

What the **f*ck** is investing?

$$\textit{Retained profit per share} = \$0.834\ USD - \$0.25\ USD = \$0.584\ USD$$

Divide the retained profit by the earnings per share:

$$\textit{Retention ratio} = \frac{\$0.584\ USD}{\$0.834\ USD} = 0.7$$

We now need to calculate the return on equity. From the income statement, the profit figure was $635 million USD and the net assets were $8,613 million USD. Divide the profits by the net assets:

$$\textit{Return on equity} = \frac{\$635\ million\ USD}{\$8,613\ million\ USD} = 0.074 = 7.4\%$$

Multiply the two together to get the sustainable growth rate:

$$\textit{Sustainable growth rate} = 7.4 * 0.7 = 5.18\%$$

For simplicity, we will round the sustainable growth rate down to 5%.

We now need to pick a discount rate. 9.2% is the figure we've been using as the annual returns of the S&P 500 so let's use that here too. When you put these numbers into a DCF calculator such as the one at www.wtfinvesting.com, you get a value per share of $29.96 USD.

In this type of analysis, you can be more conservative in your calculations by reducing the growth rates. If you think a company is going to grow at a higher rate than its five year average then you can put in higher figures too. Try doing both; it will give you a value range that you might expect the stock price to achieve.

To do this for Newcrest, set the long term growth rate to 0% and the short term rate to 13.6% to get a low estimate. You could then set the long term growth rate to 5% and short term growth rate to 16% to get a top estimate. If you do this, you get a range of $15.87 - $33.06 USD.

Compare that to the current market price of $18.31 USD and you can see that the company is trading under our top estimate of its value. The thing you could do now is really check and double check your growth and discount figures and make sure you are comfortable with them.

You should then look at the company's strategic position before making a final decision on whether the company is a good investment at the current price.

So why is this so different to the other methods? Well firstly, the DCF method is the only method that accounts for potential growth in its valuation. It also takes into account the revenue generated from assets which the first method doesn't do.

This valuation method also doesn't use an arbitrary comparison to other companies. It is a much more useful method of calculating the intrinsic value of a company than the first two methods. Sure, the first two methods will definitely give you an indication of whether a company is undervalued but they can't give you an idea of whether a company is overvalued. The DCF method on the other hand, can give an indication of either.

Considering the strategic position of company

Now that you have three different valuations using these three different methods, you need to add in some more

What the **f*ck** is investing?

information about the company's strategic position to see whether you think the company is a good investment. When doing this, you should consider the wider markets that the company is involved in. In this case, as a metal mining company, the price of gold and copper will heavily influence its share price.

At the time of writing, uncertainty caused by the global pandemic and record levels of quantitative easing (money printing) is pushing the gold price up. At the same time, record demand for copper because of things like the boom in electric vehicle demand and production is pushing the price of copper up. You should consider the likelihood of the prices of these commodities rising in the long term and how this will affect the company's share price. This can be clearly seen on Newcrest's income statement above, the realised price of gold Newcrest achieved between 2019 and 2020 rose by 21%. This could explain the rise in profits between those years of 15%. At the same time, the company has other strategic development plans under its control. It has multiple exploration projects and new mines coming online that will provide additional assets and sources of income for the company.

The cost of actually mining is also a big variable the company can control; is the company innovating and reducing these costs? Are the new development projects likely to become successful mines? You can see Newcrest reduced the all in sustaining cost of producing gold and copper by 17% between 2019 and 2020. This would also have influenced that rise in profits. You can see why these are all good questions to consider and add in to your company valuation.

Another useful thing to consider is to find out what institutional investors are doing. Remember that on the other side of every share you buy is a seller. Imagine that the seller is an institutional investor; what do they know about this stock that you don't know? This is why it is also useful to look up what kind of organisations are holding shares in the company you are looking at. Are a large proportion of the shares held by institutional investors? If not, why not? You can also look and see whether these institutions are increasing their holdings in the company or reducing their holdings. Do this by comparing the ownership figures over the last six months or so. If institutions are increasing their positions, it shows professional investors have looked at the company and consider it to be a good investment. If they are reducing their positions it could mean the opposite.

When you have considered your value estimate as well as the strategic position of the company, you will have a very clear view of whether the company is a good investment or not. In the case of our example company, Newcrest, given the value we got out of our DCF analysis, the rising price of gold during this period of economic uncertainty, the multiple development projects the company has ongoing and the companies good record of reducing its running costs, I would definitely consider it a contender for a place in my portfolio before discounting for any wider risks the company faces.

Key points to remember

A good thing to be aware of is the fact that financial markets can be irrational. You could get the value of an investment spot on but at the end of the day, the market still may not value it the same as you. You need to consider how much risk is involved in an investment and compare it to your expected returns.

What the **f*ck** is investing?

You will need to decide whether that level of risk is acceptable for the returns you might expect. Try and think of factors that would affect your investment both within the company and in the wider market. Sense check any assumptions you have made when calculating your valuations.

You can also increase your discount rate in our DCF analysis to take an element of risk into account. In our Newcrest example, increase the discount rate from 9.2% to 11.2% to take into account risks we haven't predicted. You'll see our top end valuation goes down to $20.07. You can see how important this is and how it might influence your decision to invest.

Remember, it's possible to lose all your money if you get it wrong so make sure you take the time to check your research and ask for professional help if you are still not sure. Make sure your emotions are not guiding any of your decision making and if necessary, sleep on any decision before you make it.

When picking investments, it is easy to get drawn into hype or the fear of missing out on big gains. It is important not to make rash decisions. Don't try and chase quick rises on stocks you haven't researched. If you see a stock rise sharply in price, you have already missed it so don't try and chase quick wins. If you wouldn't own a stock for 5 years, don't own it for a day. Don't try to time the market; gains are made through time in the market, not timing the market.

You should also prepare yourself for the realities of the ups and downs of investing. Markets fluctuate and some days your investments might go down in value. You need to keep calm and remember that if the fundamentals of your investment haven't changed, then the price at that time doesn't matter. Investors who think and stay invested over long periods usually do better than those who try to trade often

Chapter 5:
Investment strategies

Before you run off and start buying investments, you should have an overall investment strategy that is tailored to you and your own goals. There are many strategies out there that you could employ, I've picked some of the most important and powerful ones.

Value investing

Value investing is a strategy some of the most successful investors use. Value is a simple concept; find companies whose shares are trading at a discount to their intrinsic value and buy their shares. The hope is that the share price will return to their intrinsic value and you can then sell them and make a profit. It sounds simple; all you need to know is the company's share price and its value. As we have already learned however, valuing companies is not easy and there is no correct answer or method.

There can be a lot of reasons why a company's shares trade at a discount to their value; a company might release unfavourable news that the market overreacts to or they might have cut their dividend. All you need to know is that markets can be irrational and don't always value companies at what they should be worth. Of course this irrationality can both help us and hinder us.

There is a saying in the investing world; the market can be wrong for longer than you can be solvent. With that warning in mind, the important thing to remember about value investing is that it most often outperforms other strategies when used over a long period of time.

When looking for companies to buy as part of a value investing strategy, on top of your DCF valuation, the key metrics you should be interested in are P/B ratio, P/E ratio and free cash flow. For P/B and P/E ratios, you want to see a value as close to 1 as possible, ideally below 1. A P/B ratio of 1 indicates that the company's market value is equal to the total value of its assets. If the P/B ratio is less than 1, it means the company's total assets are worth more than the current share price. This is a good signal that a company is undervalued as in principle, even if the company was liquidated, it's assets would still be worth more than the price paid at that time.

A P/E ratio of 1 indicates that a company's market value is equal to its earnings. As far as free cash flow goes, you want to find companies with plenty of free cash flow that they could use to reinvest in the business, pay dividends or buy back shares. All of these are likely to lead to an increase in the share price in future.

Dividend investing

Dividend investing is useful for anyone that wants a regular income from their investments. It involves identifying investments that pay regular, reliable dividends and buying their shares. Dividend investing can be useful as your shares can gain from your shares rising in value as well as from the dividend payments. Income from dividends is also taxed at a favourable rate when compared to other income sources in some countries and so it can be a tax efficient income stream for many investors.

Dividend investors are generally less concerned with fluctuations in the share price of a company and more about the reliability of the dividends payment and growth. Of course share price is important when investing for dividends; the share price will affect the dividend return or yield. The dividend yield is simply the share price divided by the dividend paid.

There are two approaches investors can take when investing for dividends; investing for high dividend yield and investing for high dividend growth. Investing for high dividend yield is buying companies who pay the biggest dividends. Investing for high dividend growth is buying companies who do not necessarily pay large dividends now but have a lot of potential to grow and pay larger dividends in the future. As dividend paying investments tend to be more defensive and stable companies, they tend to be less volatile in their price.

When choosing companies for a dividend investing strategy, you are interested in the company's profitability and how likely the company is to stay profitable. Look at the percentage of total profits that the company is paying as dividends. 30-40% is considered to be about right. Any higher and the company might put its future profitability at risk as it cannot invest as much in sustaining its own growth and efficiency. Also look at the historic profitability of the company. Have the company's annual profits been stable or volatile? Volatility in profits year to year suggests its dividends might not be reliable. Consider any dividend payments the company has made in previous years. Are they reliable, have they grown from year to year? Finally, consider the value of the company. There is little point in investing in a company with a good reliable dividend if the share price is double what its valuation suggests it should be.

Growth investing

Growth investing is a strategy that involves buying shares in companies companies that have the potential to grow at higher rate than the market average. Growth companies could be relatively young companies or they could be companies trying to make a big breakthrough that could lead to them making big profits in future. Growth investing can be riskier than other strategies as the companies tend to be less mature and often don't have established products or income.

Growth companies could also be in industries that are experiencing booms fuelled by speculation. The risk is that these booms turn to busts. The dot com bubble is a classic example of this. In the early 2000's excessive speculation in internet related companies ended with a stock market crash where a lot of internet related companies failed and shut down.

Growth investing is a good strategy for potentially making large profits but it is important to manage the risk it plays in your investments. Research is as important as ever here and it is important not to get drawn in by hype around these investments. Remember that our goal is to invest and not speculate. The fear of missing out with growth stocks can often be dangerous and so you should try and recognise when your emotions are influencing your decision making.

When trying to identify companies who have the potential for higher than average growth, you should look at previous

What the **f*ck** is investing?

year's earnings as well as potential future earnings. You want to see companies who increase their earnings year on year. You also want to see this earnings growth being predicted to continue by company analysts. Profit margins that increase year to year as well as a return on equity that increases year to year both indicate that the company may be controlling its costs efficiently as well as generating more sales. The sustainable growth rate figure is important to look at when investing for growth. If a company is growing at less than its sustainable rate, it indicates that the company has capacity to grow at a higher rate in future.

Investment strategy comparison

	DIVIDEND STOCKS	VALUE STOCKS	GROWTH STOCKS
Investment Horizon	Short to long term	Mid to long term	Mid to long term
Risk Level	Lower	Medium	High
Valuation	Fair	Undervalued	Overvalued
Growth Potential	Low	Medium	High
Maket Cap	Mid – large cap	Mid – large cap	Small – large cap
Pays Dividends?	Yes	Yes	No

Goals, Risk tolerance, time horizon

In order to choose an investment strategy, you need to set goals and define our risk tolerance and time horizon.

The first thing you should do is set some goals. What is your ultimate goal? Is it to retire completely? Or reduce your hours? Or start your own business? This goal could be anything but you ultimately should have a realistic goal to work towards. Once you have your goal, you need to know how much money you would need to achieve that goal. You should already have an idea of how much money you need to live on after reading chapter one. This is the amount you will need your investments to pay you in order to be free to pursue our goal. Of course if your goal actually generates an income, you can include this in your calculation as it will reduce the amount your investments need to generate.

Calculating how much you need

According to Goldman-Sachs the average 10 year stock market return over the past 140 years has been 9.2%. If you have a properly diversified portfolio, you should be able to use this as a guide to how much you can expect your investments in the stock market to return on average. First you should adjust this value for inflation; you don't want to allow inflation to erode the value of your investments. The average inflation rate in the UK since 1980 has been 2.51% so we will use that (You can look up the average rate for your country online). Subtract that inflation rate from your expected return rate and we get; 9.2 – 2.51 = 6.69. Of course, depending on where you live, you will need to consider tax. You should add your tax rate onto your annual expenses. If your tax rate is 20% for example, multiply your annual expenses by 1.2. Divide your annual expenses including tax by 6.69 and then multiply by 100. This is how much money you will need to be financially independent and pursue your goals. For example, if your annual expenses including tax are £25,000, you will need; 25,000/6.69 *100 = £373,692. You

    What the **f*ck** is investing?

can also enter these numbers into the free calculator at www.wtfinvesting.com.

Try the calculation for yourself, you can play it safer if you prefer by assuming a lower rate of return but try not to assume you will beat the market every year. It is best to be conservative, that way you are less likely to underestimate the time you'll need or the amount you need to invest. Ultimately the returns you expect are an important consideration and they are directly linked to your appetite for risk or risk tolerance. It is important to understand your risk tolerance and manage it when necessary.

As a rule of thumb, the closer you are to your financial goals, the less risk tolerant you should be. The total you came up with above as well as the amount of time you have to achieve it will govern how much risk you are prepared to take on. If you assumed you had 20 years, you started with £1000 and saved £200 per month and your annual return is 9.2%. The amount you would have after 20 years is £144,324. So to reach the goal of £373,692 in this case you would need to either start with more money, save more money per month or achieve a higher return. You should try and influence all three by investing more and by making better investment decisions.

Use the free compound interest calculator at www.wtfinvesting.com and plug your own numbers into it. You will get an idea for how much you will need to invest to achieve your goal. Remember also that as you create more streams of income and improve your money management as we discussed in chapter one, your capacity to invest will increase and your goals will be easier and quicker to achieve.

Asset allocation

As part of your investment strategy, you need to consider your asset allocation. This essentially means not putting all your eggs in one basket. You should consider splitting your investments across different investment types as a way of managing risk. For example, you could decide to allocate a third of your portfolio to stocks, a third to mutual funds and a third to bonds. Your asset management plan will mostly be governed by your appetite for risk and reward.

If you favour less risk and are happy with less reward, you could have more long term bonds in your portfolio. If you want to simply protect your assets from inflation, you might have a larger portion of gold in your portfolio. If you want to prioritise maximum potential returns and are comfortable with a larger amount of risk, you could allocate a larger portion of your portfolio to stocks. If you have a long period of time in which to build your investments, you might allocate a larger portion of your portfolio to index funds. Use the graph below to compare investment types and their expected risks and returns.

Risk — return graph

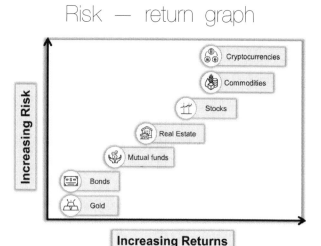

What the f*ck is investing?

There is no correct answer to asset allocation but you'll be able to find plenty of suggestions online but always remember to adjust for your own circumstances. You can use the matrix below to compare the investment types. It shows what economic climates each type of investment performs best in. A good strategy is to have investments that come under each of the four quadrants of the matrix. This spreads risk and increases the chances that your investments will perform in all economic climates.

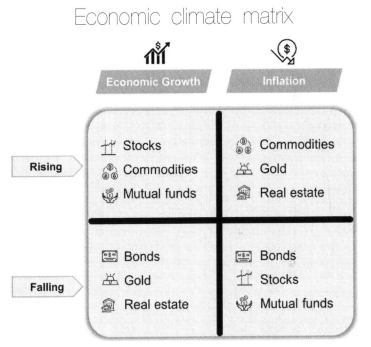

As well as managing risk in different economic climates with your asset allocation as discussed above, something you should really consider when thinking about asset allocation is your level of investing experience. There is little point in allocating a third of your overall portfolio to stocks when you are brand new to investing. This would be exceptionally risky to do unless you had really spent the time learning what to do.

I've seen a lot of statistics suggesting that on average private investors lose money in the stock market. I've no way of verifying these so I haven't quoted them but it is a topic I often see coming up on investing news articles. The premise is that most people will buy stocks without having done appropriate research or not understanding the investment. It continues to say that had they simply bought an index fund, they would have made that average return from the stock market of 9.2% instead of losing money.

We have no way of knowing whether most private investors lose in the stock market or not but I can easily believe it. This is why I believe that new investors should allocate a much larger portion of their portfolios to diversified assets like mutual funds until they have built enough knowledge to make solid stock picking decisions. Consider starting your portfolio off with quality mutual funds whilst you build your investing knowledge and experience.

Chapter 6:
Put it all into practise

Now that you know how to research your investments and have put together an investment strategy, you now need to find out the most efficient way for you to invest. Different investment accounts with different providers all have advantages and disadvantages. Usually the choice of account is a very individual one and will vary from person to person based on their circumstances and preferences. It is a subject that should be carefully considered. In some countries, private investors can open tax efficient investing accounts. In the UK for example, this is called a Stocks and Shares ISA.

The tax implications of using a standard account when you could have used an ISA are potentially huge. You should check what accounts are available in your country and consider the tax implications of each type. The first type of account you should consider is a tax efficient account (Stocks and Shares ISA in the UK) and then a standard investing account. Contract for difference or leveraged accounts should be avoided unless you are very experienced and understand exactly what you are doing. Whatever account you end up opening, ensure the provider is regulated by the appropriate financial regulator in your country. Common types of investment accounts are listed below.

Tax efficient accounts

If you live in the UK like me, and you want to invest in stocks, funds and ETF's, you can make your investments in a Stocks and Shares ISA. Other countries do have similar accounts and it is well worth checking to see what tax efficient investment accounts are available in your country. Most countries have accounts that have certain tax advantages and could keep some of your investments safe from the tax man. It is absolutely essential to consider this point at the start of your investing career. The tax man could end up taking a large chunk of your hard earned investments if you don't take full advantage of any tax breaks your country offers.

The UK Stocks and shares ISA for example, is a nice tax free wrapper you can pay up to £20,000 per tax year into. This means that you can invest up to £20,000 a year and any capital gains or dividends received as long as they are made within the account, are tax free. In principle, over the years you could build up millions worth on investments in a Stocks and Shares ISA and at the time of writing, you wouldn't pay a penny of tax on any of it.

There is one caveat to that in the UK. You will still have to pay 15% tax on any gains from stocks listed in the United States. There are many providers of these accounts in the UK each with advantages and disadvantages. Some providers charge annual fees and most will charge a fee for every trade made. It is a good idea to compare these accounts to get an idea of the fees you will pay every year.

Standard investing accounts

If you live in the UK and have not used all of your annual ISA allowance, you should consider a Stocks and Shares

What the f*ck is investing?

ISA instead of a standard investment account. If you do not have a tax efficient account available in your country or you have used all your allowances for the tax year, a standard investment account is something you should consider.

The process for choosing a provider is the same as choosing a provider for an ISA account. For investors in other countries, nearly all will have standard investing accounts if they don't have tax efficient accounts.

Contract for difference (CFD) accounts

Another type of account you can open is a CFD account. This is something I would avoid as a general rule. Trading CFD's is a good way to lose a lot of money fast, especially if you are inexperienced. CFD's in my opinion are speculative; as the trader is betting that the price of a stock or security will either go up or go down within a period of time often based on analysis of charts and trends.

A Contract for Difference is a contract between a buyer and seller that says that the buyer must pay the difference between the current value of an asset and the future value of an asset at the time the contract is settled. If the difference is negative, the seller instead pays the buyer. In a nutshell, the trader who is buying the CFD is essentially speculating on whether the price of an asset is going to go up or down. If they are correct, they will profit, if not they will lose money.

A CFD trader never actually owns the underlying asset but benefits or loses based on the price change of the asset. Where CFD's get dangerous for inexperienced traders is that they often use leverage. Leverage is essentially the use of debt to increase the capital used in an investment. With CFD's the leverage can often go as high as 50:1. This means that the trader "borrows" £50 for every £1 they invest. Whilst this obviously can lead to higher returns, it can also lead to large losses.

Let's take the example of a trader who enters a "buy" contract that has leverage of 50:1 with £1000. The stock price at the time of entering the contract is £10. You can think of it as if the trader has "bought" £50,000 worth or 5000 shares of the stock. If the stock price moves up 2% to £10.20, the trader could make £1000 profit (5000 * £10.20 = £51,000). If the stock price moved the other way and down 2% however, the story is different. The trader will lose their entire investment (5000 * £9.80 = £49,000). In reality, most CFD providers actually require a deposit called "margin" in order to open and maintain CFD positions. If the margin is 20% in this case, it means that the stock's price would only have to drop by 1.6% in order for the traders' position to be closed at a loss of £800. Small fluctuations in a securities price can have huge impacts on CFD and leveraged investments.

It is no coincidence that when you are signing up to a CFD account in the UK, the broker is required to put warnings to investors about the high likelihood of them losing money. One popular CFD trading platform has a warning "76% of retail investors lose money when trading with this provider". This isn't unique to that one provider, other providers I looked at provided similar figures for the proportion of people that lose money. Trading with leverage is risky and evidently, most people lose money doing it.

The fact that the Financial Conduct Authority in the UK has had to act to regulate the industry because so many retail investors were losing money tells its own story.

What the **f*ck** is investing?

Don't overestimate your abilities and assume that you will make it into the minority that make money using this type of account. Be honest with yourself, if you're not an experienced investor, stick to regular unleveraged investing accounts.

Practise money account

A practise trading account is a great way to get used to a new broker or investing as a whole before committing your money. A practise account will allow you to use "practise money" to place practise trades and get used to how the market works. Practise money accounts are good for getting used to the actual practise of making a trade if you have never done it before.

You could potentially be investing large sums of money with each real trade costing you. Using a practise account to get used to placing market orders is highly recommended. A decimal point in the wrong place could cost dearly on a real money account for example. When it comes to placing your first real trade, you will be much less likely to make a mistake that could cost you money.

Some brokers also offer bespoke educational resources for people using their practise accounts. This is a great way to take advantage of free resources to help you in your investment research. You can even practise your investing strategies using a practise account before committing real money.

Providers

Choosing a broker is also an important thing to consider. Each broker is different and will have different advantages and disadvantages. Some brokers for example, will charge an annual account fee, others will charge larger fees per trade and some will give you access to more markets and investments than others. Some brokers also offer free trading but you should always remember that there is no such thing as a free lunch, you are paying somewhere along the way.

With free trading brokers, they often make money in having larger spreads than other brokers. Whether you choose a free trade account or not would be influenced on how often you plan on trading. I would suggest that as you should be aiming to trade less often and hold investments for longer, trading fees are less important in that case.   Some good things to compare are the ease of use of the brokers' platform, the research resources it provides to you and the overall number and quality of investments it allows you to access.

Some providers charge annual fees on their accounts. Comparing any fees can save you a lot of money in the long run as these fees can have a big impact on how much of your investments you get to keep. An uncapped annual fee is something I would look to avoid. If your account grows a lot in value which is your aim, you would end up paying big fees if you do not shop around for the best account. A 0.5% fee might seem insignificant but for investing, you need to look at the long term. I can demonstrate just how much a seemingly small fee can affect your long term investment using the following example.

Imagine two people both opened an investment account with $10,000. Each person contributes $200 per month to their account over 20 years. Each account returns an average of 5% per year before fees. Now if we say that one account has had an annual fee of 0.5% and the other had an annual fee of 1.5%, the difference in their account value after 20 years is huge. The account with the fee of 0.5% would be worth $102,796 whereas the account with the 1.5% fee would be worth $90,144. That's a difference of $12,652 or difference in overall return of 12%!

So you can see how those seemingly small fees are incredibly important to keep an eye on. This doesn't just apply to accounts as well. Remember that some actively managed investments such as certain mutual funds also have fees. Make sure you pay attention to fees and minimise them if you possibly can.

If you plan on trading often for example, a provider with a lower trading fee might be a good choice. If you don't plan on trading often or plan on using the maximum ISA allowance every year, an account with a lower annual fee might be right for you. Some brokers provide research resources and some have nicer, easier to use apps or platforms. The choice is down to your individual preferences. It is worth noting that you can always transfer to a different provider in the next tax year if you are not happy.

When you start looking for a broker, you will quickly find that there are a lot of options to choose from. Luckily, to help narrow down the list, there are comparison sites that allow you to compare brokers in a similar way to comparison sites we discussed in the first chapter. Go to www.wtfinvesting.com where I have listed brokers you can use in your country. When you have narrowed down the list, it is a good idea to make use of a practise money account if offered by any of the brokers. This will give you a chance to actually try the brokers' platform out for as long as you need before actually committing any money to that platform.

Security is another aspect to consider when looking at brokers. You don't want your money to be vulnerable with a broker that has lax IT security in place. Your broker should use technologies such as two factor authentication and encryption as standard. Two factor authentication for example, means that someone can't log into your account with your password alone. This is important as online passwords are notoriously weak and easily compromised. The added layer of security makes it a lot less likely that someone could access your account and steal your money. One of the most important points to look into is whether the broker is regulated by the financial regulator in your country. For example, In the UK, this would be the Financial Conduct Authority (FCA) and in the USA, it would be the Financial Industry Regulatory Authority (FINRA). It is absolutely essential that you check what the appropriate authority is in your own country. You should then be able to check with the regulator that the broker you are considering is regulated by that regulator.

The FINRA in the USA for example makes this easy as it provides a website where you can search for companies that the regulator covers. Most regulators should provide an easy way of checking your broker with them. If you are planning on buying certificates of deposit or saving with your broker, you should also check that any financial services compensation scheme in your country covers them. These schemes guarantee deposits up to a certain value in the event of your broker going bust. Ensuring your broker is a regulated and reputable organisation is absolutely essential as you could be depositing a lot of money through them in your investing career.

Finally, it is worth saying that if you find that you are not happy with the service your broker is offering, it is possible to switch to a new broker without having to sell your investments. You can simply transfer your investments from one broker to another. This is called an "in specie"

What the **f*ck** is investing?

transfer. This is important to remember because if you sell your investments in order to move to a new broker and buy them back, you could lose money through in trading fees, differences in market prices and most importantly, you could incur a big capital gains liability as soon as you sell. Ask your current broker how to make this transfer and they should be able to help you through the process.

Making the trade

Now you should be able to put together a great financial plan, research the investments that fit this plan and find a broker that suits you. Your financial plan is working and you now have spare cash to invest so, how do you actually make the trade or buy investments? You should have an idea of the price you want to either buy or sell your investment for. The next step is actually executing the order.

Bid and ask

When placing trades you will notice some extra terms around the window that need explained. The bid price is the highest price a buyer is currently willing to pay and the ask price is the lowest price a seller is currently willing to accept for a security. The difference between these two numbers is known as the spread. Generally speaking, the lower the spread, the more liquid the security and therefore the easier it is for an investor to either build a position or liquidate a position. Something to be wary of is stocks that suffer from very low liquidity. Low liquidity stocks can make it hard for an investor to liquidate their position. You can essentially get stuck with the security because no one is willing to buy.

There are four different types of orders you can make for both buying and selling stocks, shares, bonds and funds.

These are market orders, limit orders, stop orders and stop limit orders.

Market orders

Market orders are executed at the best currently available market prices. You can either set the amount of money you want to invest or the number of shares you want to buy and your broker will execute the order at the best price it can get at that time. Market orders have the benefit you are almost guaranteed your order will be executed as long as there are buyers and sellers. The downside is that the price you pay when the order is executed may not be the price you expected. In times of high volatility, there's a chance that the price you get is significantly different to what you expected. This is why in most cases; you should use a limit order instead. You should only use a market order when you want the order executed quickly at any cost or when you're trading a low number of shares.

Limit orders

A limit order allows you to set the maximum price you are willing to pay for a share if buying or the minimum price you are willing to accept if selling. Limit orders protect you from paying too much or getting too little in periods of volatility. The downside of a limit order is that there is no guarantee that your order will be executed. If you set a minimum price you're willing to pay for a stock, there's no guarantee that the price will go down to that price for the order to be executed. You should use a limit order when you want to specify a price you want to buy or sell at or you're trading a large number of shares. In most cases, as we are long term investors, this is the type of trade we should be using.

 What the **f*ck** is investing?

Stop orders

A stop order allows you to set a price above or below the current price which converts your order to a market order. As this kind of stop order is filled at the market price, it has the same drawbacks that a market order has. Your price target price could be hit, converting your order to a market order, the price could then move in an unfavourable direction and your order would still be fulfilled. Again, the benefit of this is that you are much more likely to have your order executed in the event of your price target being triggered at the risk of getting a less favourable price. You should use a stop order when you want to protect a short or long position from losses above a set level. This type of order is more useful to higher frequency traders, if you're a long term investor you probably don't need to use this type of order.

Stop limit orders

A stop limit order on the other hand allows you to set a price above or below the current market price which converts your order to a limit order. This limit order then protects you if the price moves in an unfavourable direction after your target price is hit. As with any limit order, there is no guarantee that it will be executed when your target price is hit but the limit order protects you from potentially getting a less favourable price than you are willing to accept. Stop limit orders are used in similar situations to stop orders. In this case you use a stop limit order when you want to specify a price that you must get once your price target is reached. This type of order is also more useful to higher frequency traders, if you're a long term investor you probably don't need to use this type of order.

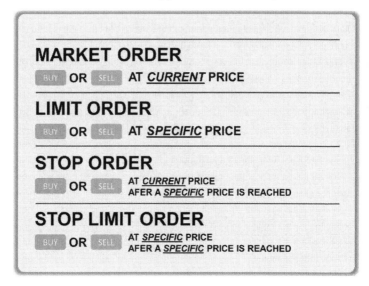

MARKET ORDER

BUY OR SELL AT _CURRENT_ PRICE

LIMIT ORDER

BUY OR SELL AT _SPECIFIC_ PRICE

STOP ORDER

BUY OR SELL AT _CURRENT_ PRICE
AFER A _SPECIFIC_ PRICE IS REACHED

STOP LIMIT ORDER

BUY OR SELL AT _SPECIFIC_ PRICE
AFER A _SPECIFIC_ PRICE IS REACHED

Order example

To put all this into practise, you can run through the example of buying a stock using a limit order. Let's suppose you have decided that we want to buy shares in Apple and you have $1000 dollars to invest in this stock.

The current stock price is $128.91.

You could either place a limit order for 7 shares with the limit price being $128.91.

This would execute assuming the price stayed at or below this level and the trade would cost you a total of 7 *128.91 = $902.37 not including any taxes.

This means you have bought 7 shares for $902.37 and have $97.63 left over. If for example, you didn't want to pay above $125 per share, you could place a limit order for 8 shares with the limit price being $125.

If the stock price went down to $125 or below before the order expired, the order would execute costing you 8 *$125 = $1000. You would have just bought 8 shares costing a total of $1000 with $0 left over.

Suppose your order executed as per the second example. You now own 8 shares that cost $125 each. Now, consider the situation a year later if the price of that stock had risen to $150 per share.

You might want to protect any profits you have made. Now for example, you could place a stop-limit order to sell all 8 of your shares at a price of $135 if the share price drops to $140.

This means that if the share price dropped to between $135 and $140, your order would execute if buyers were available. This order would be protecting between $10 and $15 per share profit. Open a practise account and practise using the different types of orders before trying it with real money.

Closing remarks

You have now made the first step in becoming a successful investor. Those couple of hours invested reading may be the most important investment you make. It is just the start of your journey.

Remember that investing is a broad subject and it will take some time to get your head around all the concepts. Read this book again if you have to. Make use of the summary diagrams and tables to help you along the way and make use of the resources online at www.wtfinvesting.com.

The better your understanding of the basics, the more likely you are to succeed. I have suggested more advanced reading for when you are ready on the website above. It will continually be updated with useful tools, links, research suggestions and you can even reach out to me personally there. Tell me your story and keep me updated on your journey into investing.

You now have the knowledge to separate the link between your time and your money.

You now know how to manage money, value investments and make investments. You don't have to count on a lottery win anymore!

About the author

Self-improvement and investing have been of interest since Alastair graduated from University of Liverpool. A professional engineer by day, Alastair is a Chartered Engineer with the Royal Aeronautical Society. His profession involves taking complex ideas and information and communicating them in a better way; something reflected in his book "What the f*ck is investing?" He grew up on the North Coast of Ireland before moving to England where he now lives with his girlfriend and their daughter.

Connect with Alastair at www.wtfinvesting.com

If you found this book helpful, please leave a review HERE so that more people can find this book.

Manufactured by Amazon.ca
Bolton, ON